Star Dancer

By

B.N. Rundell

Chapter 1: Daydreaming

THE WIND RIVER MOUNTAIN range bordered the Western horizon with scallops of white on the crystal blue of the cloudless sky. Dropping their dark blue skirts to the hint of spring greening on the foothills below, the mountains beckoned to the wanderlust of Trey Standingelk, who spent as much time gazing at the distant mountains as he did poring over his schoolbooks. No matter what class required his presence, he always sought a seat near the window and if the buildings of the Wyoming High School obscured his view of the mountains, he sated his hunger for freedom with oft-repeated daydreams or reminiscences of past excursions into the Bridger Wilderness area. Images of bugling bull elk with their antlers laid back along their rumps and their pawing of the ground to challenge other bulls for the superiority of the forest, or of startled mule deer bounding across a grassy meadow, or even a massive grizzly bear lumbering through the trails of the towering ponderosa pines as if he owned the forest, all instilling in him the determination to join them in the mountains as soon as the slow arriving spring melted the mountain snow.

The rattle of the bell stirred Trey from his reverie and made the announcement of the noon hour. More of a loner than most, Trey did not relish the time in the school cafeteria with the crowd and din of his fellow students. He reluctantly made his way through the corridors to the large sunlit cafeteria and followed the line to pick up the necessary tray and the accompanying utensils for his lunch meal. As he shuffled along the line, sliding his lunch tray on the pipe serving shelf and picking his portions for lunch, his desire was to be as inconspicuous as possible. He didn't like crowds and liked the noise even less, but as the exuberant chatter of the many students seemed to rise as he approached the end of the line, he sought a quiet corner for some degree of solitude. As he scanned the cafeteria seating, a hand filled his peripheral vision as it slammed down on the corner of his tray, knocking it from his grasp and spilling the contents to the floor.

With a boisterous laugh, the perpetrator yelled, "Hey, lookee here, Trey spilled his tray! Ain't that just like a dummy? Can't do anything right!" He laughed again and turned to his three companions as they joined him in the ridicule. This had become an all too common occurrence in the mind of Trey but he forced himself to walk away from the group, leaving the mess where it lay. "Hey dummy, don't walk away and leave this mess. You're sposed to clean it up!" yelled the ringleader of the turmoil. He was Mark Blackman, a senior and the captain of the Chiefs basketball team, and the all around big man on campus. From his 6'5" lean frame, he looked down on everyone, but from his standing on the team and his family's prominence on the reservation, he made it a point to look down on everyone in every way possible. He wasn't especially good looking, but his talent on the basketball court overcame any of his shortcomings in the appearance department, and if you didn't think he was important all you had to do was wait a bit and he would tell you just how important he was, or at least thought he was. Because his dad was on the school board and was considered a prime candidate for tribal council, the staff had a hands off approach and discipline was not often forthcoming, though well deserved. His followers were fellow team members and always followed his lead regardless where or into what mischief he took them.

As a freshman or ninth grader, Trey stood 5'6" with long straight black hair hanging down his back. At 15 he was still growing and was just starting to fill out his frame, but already showed broad shoulders and a well-tapered torso. It was evident that at full growth, he would be a sizeable man, but now walked with his head bowed and moved toward his locker in the main hallway. Middle school had been a struggle for Trey, and high school had proven to be much more of a challenge. It wasn't just the classes, but the more difficult demands on his performance and then the social part and having to relate to the many different students.

Wyoming Indian High had the usual class breakdown in students with the studious group, at the top of the list. Following that group were the athletes, basically anyone that participated in any of the athletic competitions. Then there was the crowd that was found in most schools as the group that did anything that set them apart as not belonging. Every generation had its names for those groups, but at Wyoming Indian, there were additional groups or classifications; the rodeo team or cowboys, the traditionalists or those that sought to follow the old ways, and as any new fad came along there would be other categories. However, over all these groups, unlike in an anglo or white school, was the historic division of Shoshone and Arapaho. Although not talked about openly in the administration circles, everyone knew it existed and nothing could change it. If nothing else caused a division, then anything that could be blamed on one tribal tradition or custom having preference over another with the opposing tribe, a conflict would soon show.

Trey grabbed his pack in his locker, unzipped it and stuffed his notebooks and needed texts in, slipped it over one shoulder and shut the locker door. He turned and headed for the front

3

door without looking back down the hallway as his tormentors shouted at his retreat. As he hit the broad bar to open the door, an alarm sounded and he stepped into his easy loping stride to leave the school campus. He knew he would be reported to the school office for leaving the campus without permission, but he had taken more than he could handle from the round ball crowd and he saw no reason to be subjected to any more ridicule. *I don't understand it. I did nothing to them, there is no reason for them to always harass me. I'm not taking it anymore.* Without slowing his gait, he easily covered the distance to his Grandmother's home. Because his dad worked in the oil field and was gone for weeks at a time and his mother worked as a waitress in town, Trey spent most afternoons and evenings with his maternal Grandmother, Minnie Spotted Horses. He always enjoyed his time with his Grandmother for the usual reasons that any young person favors their grandmothers, treats, encouragement, love, and time. But what he enjoyed most was the times she shared the old ways and taught him of the things that were only passed down through the oral teaching of elders. Because of her influence, Trey tried to practice the old ways as much as possible and to dress in the manner that would show his traditional leanings.

He vaulted up the steps to the doorway of his Grandmother's tribal housing home. A simple frame three bedroom similar to a tract home in an average American small town, there was no front yard or fence, but behind the home stood an aging lean-to shelter inside a small corral deep in horse manure. An older buckskin mare stood quietly on three legs with the idle hind leg propped against the other, her head hung low her ambition even lower. A saddle covered with a faded blanket straddled the three pole fence that contained the sleeping mare. With two quick knocks, Trey called out to his Grandmother and identified himself while he awaited her response. Hearing her answer from inside, he opened the door and entered the dimly lit living room. The heavy curtains kept the bright sunlight at bay as Grandmother waddled from the kitchen to receive a big hug from her favorite and only grandson. "What are you doing here at this time of day? Did you get kicked out of school?" came the inquiry from a troubled and wrinkled face topped with gray hair that hung to her shoulders in the traditional braids intertwined with colorful bits of cloth. Her flour dusted apron hung loosely from her overweight frame and foretold of some secret baked delight. Her broad smile did little to hide the tobacco stained teeth that were now well spaced across her mouth, but it did tell of the all-forgiving love she had for Trey.

"No, Grandmother, I didn't get kicked out. But it's the same old story, just because I can't read out loud like some of the others, they think I'm stupid! And they call me dummy! I can't help it!" as he voiced his frustration he ripped his pack from his shoulder and threw it in the corner of the room. "I'm no dummy! I'm just as smart as they are!"

"Why grandson, I know that. You're probably smarter than the whole lot o'them put together!" she replied with a big smile and reached out for another hug. Trey flopped down on the blanket covered couch and crossed his arms across his chest, doing his best to keep the tears locked up inside. She had heard this before, Trey had many struggles in school and most seemed to start in Middle School. Before then he had been an average student and enjoyed going to school and learning, there were some bumps in the road, especially when it came to reading, but he always managed to overcome them. Trey had shown an ability to learn and apply many common lessons of life as she taught him some of the old ways, names of plants and their uses, types of tribal ceremonies and dances, purposes of the different tribal societies. He had always been an attentive student and showed the ability to grasp the truths and applications as she patiently demonstrated them or told of them. She couldn't understand why the school teachers were not doing their job better because she knew Trey was a quick learner and a good student. "Well, let's not worry 'bout that now. Are you hungry? It's going to be a while before supper," she stated with a questioning look to her grandson.

He nodded his head and said, "Yeah, I didn't get any lunch," without explanation.

Trey's mom, Sophie, would stop by to pick him up on her way home from her work as a waitress at the restaurant in the nearby town of Lander. She would usually arrive after supper was finished and his homework was done. Usually tired from a long days work and seldom talkative, their ride home was often in total silence. As an only child, Trey spent most of his spare time with his horse, Pepper, an 8 year old paint gelding kept in a shed and corral in the back that was similar to that found at his Grandmothers. When not occupied with his horse, Trey would often watch videos of pow-wows and the different ceremonial dances. He was saving his money to purchase the necessary materials, feathers, and beads to make his own traditional ceremonial costume so he could one day participate in the dances as his Grandmother was teaching him.

Chapter 2: Suspended

SEVEN O'CLOCK WAS EARLY for the phone to be ringing in the Standingelk home and the rudely awakened Sophie feared some kind of emergency or bad news. With a tentative, "Hello" she answered the intruding telephone. Cell service was spotty in this part of the res and most homes had a traditional land line in the form of a wall phone or a bedside cradle phone. The voice at the other end spoke, "Sophie, this is Carol Knudsen at the school, I'm sorry to call so early, but I wanted to reach you before the bus came for Trey. Sophie, I'm sorry to tell you but Trey was suspended yesterday. He left the campus at noon without permission and didn't return. Our standard discipline for that is a three day suspension. So, Trey won't be able to return until next Wednesday. O.K.?" Not receiving any response, she continued, "Do you have any questions?"

Sophie muttered an answering, "Uh, no, I guess not. Next Wednesday, you say?"

"Umhumm, that's right. Next Wednesday. O.K., then, I'll let you go. Bye now,"

"Trey, get in here!" she shouted. When he appeared at her doorway in his briefs and a t-shirt, with his dog, Tobey, standing quietly by his side, she loudly asked, "Why didn't you tell me you were suspended?"

"Suspended? I didn't know. Nobody said anything to me. I didn't do nuthin' wrong," came the innocent reply.

"She said you were suspended for three days because you left the campus without permission. What's that all about?"

He stepped to her bedside and sat with one leg crooked under him, turning to face his mom. "It's the same ol' thing, Mom. Just like in Middle School. The ball players, I told you about 'em, start their garbage tryin' to make themselves look tough, harass anybody that's different from them. Yesterday, they were at the end of the line in the cafeteria, knocked my tray outta my hands and laughed about it. I didn't start it! Then they started callin' me names, like dummy. It's not my fault!" he pleaded, as he looked at his mother.

"But your suspension is because you left the school. Was that what it was about?"

"Yeah, I just couldn't take it anymore, and I knew you didn't want me fighting, so I just left," he responded with a bit of a pout. "I'd like to knock that Blackman on . . . "

"None of that. You know I'm going to have to talk to your father about this," she said. Both of them knew that Stoney, his father, would not be happy about it and would probably say he should have fought with them. His way was always, *"Be a man about it. I don't want a crybaby for a son."* His dad worked in the oil field and was seldom home and when he was, there always seemed to be a fight about something. Trey preferred to absent himself from the home to try to keep peace in the family, but he also had difficulty dealing with the noise of an argument and the yelling always caused him to tense up to the point he couldn't even move.

"Well, he won't be home for several days, and we'll deal with it then. You're going to have to fend for yourself, because I'm working every day through the weekend, so you better stay out of trouble. I'll call Grandmother and let her know you won't be coming over. This would be a good time to clean your room and maybe even the tack shed out back so your horse would have a little shelter. Now, go on and get out of here so I can get a little more sleep. I don't have to be at work for another four hours," she instructed.

Tobey followed Trey back to his room and lay down on his makeshift bed made from an old blanket. As he curled up, he dropped his head but lifted his sad-looking eyes to Trey and watched as Trey started getting dressed. Under the watchful eyes of Tobey, Trey began the process of cleaning his room, picking up the scattered dirty clothes, putting his footgear in the small closet, picking up the dirty dishes from the late night snacks, and discarding the assorted papers and other trash. Going to the kitchen to get a broom and dustpan, he passed the small dining alcove window on the back side of the house. With a casual glance outside, he was reminded of his mother's instruction to also clean the tack shed and corral. With a short whistle to Tobey, the two left the house by the back door and walked to the corral.

When the screen door slapped shut, Pepper lifted his head and nickered to Trey and Tobey. The three were often thought to be the inseparable trio that explored the wilderness at every opportunity. The horse pressed his chest to the top rail and stretching his neck over the fence, he mouthed his lips looking for a treat. Trey had grabbed an apple treat from the bowl by the door and now laid it in his open palm to extend the offering to Pepper. With a typical move of just his lips, Pepper made the treat disappear and with a nod of his head expressed his thanks. Trey rubbed the horse's head and spoke to him, "Hey, buddy. How ya doin'? Miss me didja? Well pretty soon we'll hit the trail and get outta this place. I guess you're wantin' to get to the mountains just as bad as I am, aren't cha?" With a last rub behind Pepper's ears, Trey stepped to the gate and started for the tack shed. Before he entered the shed, a voice called from the back door.

"I'm headed out to work, Trey. Don't forget to finish your room. I'll be a little later tonite, so don't worry 'bout me, O.K.?

9

Love ya!" The screen door slapped shut and his mother was gone. *Sure, see ya, Mom.* Trey thought as he turned to his work of cleaning up the shed. The work wasn't hard, but it was dirty. Dust was a common enemy of any effort at cleanliness, with little vegetation and a lot of wind, the area around Ethete, Wyoming was home to constant dust storms. Whether in the shed or even the home, dust was always present in abundance. After cleaning the shed, arranging the tack, and emptying the grain sacks into the barrels, Trey stepped outside and started raking the manure into a pile to be loaded into the wheelbarrow and taken to the compost pile. With the work complete, Trey's hunger prompted him to launch his raid of the kitchen for teenage body fuel. Carrying two pieces of his mother's left over pizza with a third hanging from his teeth, Trey flopped on the couch and picked up the remote. Before he could turn on the T.V., the front screen door banged against the door frame under the repeated knocking of a visitor. He set the two pieces on the paper plate on the coffee table, but continued to work on the third piece as he went to answer the door.

As he opened the door, his visitor, all 4'8" of a rather cute native turned to face him. "Hey cuz! Mom said she saw you over here. Why ain't you in school?" inquired Skye Bearchaser, Trey's nearest neighbor. Trey turned to look at the clock as he opened the door for her to enter, checking to see if she was missing school also. She wasn't.

"I got suspended," he growled.

"Whoooaaa, what'd ya do? Get in a fight?" she asked with a grin spreading to reveal her dimples. Skye and Trey had been neighbors all their life, she was just a year younger than Trey but had excelled at school and was now also a freshman and a classmate to her long-time neighbor. Best of friends, they often referred to each other as cuz because it seemed as if they were related. Every major event in their lives had been shared and the memories had strengthened the bond between them. Trey stood a full head taller than Skye, but she was always able to handle herself in any scrap with Trey. Her long raven-black hair was always tucked behind her ears and fell down her back to her waist. She was a frequent participant in the pow-wow dances and often took home top honors. Her costume had been her grandmother's and was a source of pride for the entire family, and her performances brought many great memories to the entire Arapaho nation.

"No, I left the campus without a pass."

"Yup. That'll do it. So, how long ya out for?"

"Three days. But with the weekend, it's like a vacation!" he laughed.

"Great! That'll fit with what I came to ask you," without waiting for a response, she continued, "You've been to the petroglyphs up past Dinwoody lake haven't you? I need to go get some pictures cuz I'm doin' a report on them. Can we go tomorrow?" she pleaded. Then flashing a smile at him, she added, " you know you want to get back up in the mountains."

"That's for sure, I'd really like to go up there to stay," he whispered. "Well, Dinwoody is too far for just a day trip, but I know where there are others that most don't know about. They're closer and we can make it there and back easy in a day. I'll have to clear it with my mom, but there shouldn't be any problem. She knows I've been there lots of times." The petroglyphs were in a secluded location on the reservation and were not normally open to any sightseers but in the many exploratory rides taken by Trey, he had seen several different petroglyphs, all of which were in uncommon locations. Although the two friends often went exploring together, this was one of the few locations visited by Trey without Skye.

With an enthusiastic, "Sure, just as long as there's plenty of petroglyphs!" Skye gave her assent to the alternate location.

"Be sure to bring a camera and some large pieces of paper to trace some of the pics. We'll leave first thing in the morning, so bring some lunch," he instructed. Then with a slight smile, "make sure it's enough for both of us."

Star Dancer

Chapter 3: Stories in Stone

PEPPER WHINNIED A GREETING to Trey when the young man exited the back door of the house, his prancing around the small corral proved that Pepper knew he was going to be freed from the constraints of the pole corral and was excited for the anticipated ride. Trey stepped through the gate to get to the tack shed and was immediately crowded by Pepper as the horse bumped him in the back with his chest and rested his head on Trey's shoulder. Pepper had eaten most of the flake of hay thrown to him by Trey and now kicked the remainder aside to again make his round of the corral. Trey brought his gear from the shed, dropped the saddle on the top rail, draped the blanket over it and turned with bridle in hand and reached for Pepper.

He led the now saddled Pepper to the front of the house and tied a rein to the tether post by the front corner of the house. Loosely looping the rein through the metal ring, he turned to see Skye approaching on her little buckskin. The two, Skye and her little mare, Praline, were well suited for one another. The buckskin was just 14 hands tall but well muscled with the usual black stockinged legs and mane and tail. She got the horse as a foal and had trained her by herself and had a special bond and communication with the mare. Trey and Skye had been on many rides together and the horses were well acquainted with one another. Waving to Skye, Trey went back into the house to retrieve his saddle bags with his lunch and canteen. Returning to the front step, he watched as Skye trotted her mare up to the step. Trey reached down and rubbed the little buckskin's head and ears and greeted his best friend. "So, you all set? "

"Just waitin' on you, slow poke," she responded with a broad smile. "Where are we going? Is this some secret location you're taking me to?"

"Not so secret. We'll follow the North Fork up towards Wolverine Mountain. We should get there about lunch time. That should give you plenty of time to check everything out."

He stepped in his stirrup to swing his leg over the saddle, turned Pepper's head around and with a little leg pressure, started West toward Ft. Washakie. Skye spurred her buckskin to move alongside the bigger paint. The horses soon matched gaits and the pair traveled the side of the dirt road towards the highway. Traffic was light and crossing the highway was easily done. A few early tourists had pulled into the storefront in search of souvenirs while the two adventurers pointed their mounts between the buildings and along the well-traveled road that led to the cemetery or the confluence of the Little Wind River and the North Fork. Taking the lead, Trey left the roadside to join a trail that followed the North Fork upstream. Although the North Fork was actually the North Fork of the Little Wind River, in many mountain areas it would be classified as more of a creek than a river. In several places the water was no more than a foot deep and in some areas the stream was barely fifteen feet across, but though small, it was considered a year round stream.

The stream side trail followed every bend of the small river but often climbed an out thrust bank or rock outcropping or twisted around a cluster of willow or an occasional small cottonwood grove. Trey and Skye were always very observant of their surroundings, often calling attention to different plants or the scrambling of a startled animal. Rounding one larger bend that was well crowded with willows, the duo startled a sizable mule deer with an impressive rack of antlers that instantly bounded up the riverbank and disappeared in the sagebrush covered flats. Just as the deer was startled, Pepper sprang backwards causing Trey to lose his seat and find himself draped over the gelding's neck with the saddle horn digging into his groin. Fortunately Pepper didn't move any further and Trey sought to regain his seat to the accompaniment of the laughter emanating from his traveling companion.

"Whoa, Cowboy! I thought we were gonna have a rodeo right here. I could just see you gettin' dumped in the water and comin' up with a nice brookie trout in your pocket! Say, mebbe you oughta try that again, a couple of brookies would make a nice lunch, dontcha think?" she chided.

"Yeah, like I'm gonna get myself bucked off just so you can have fish for dinner. I don't think that's gonna happen."

The momentary excitement broke the monotony of the trail ride and brought the attention of the riders back to the trail. Trey noticed a few areas where the Bluegrass was starting to green up and some of the creek-side moss and grasses were anticipating the coming of Spring. As the weather warmed and the high mountain snowpack melted, the stream would as much as double in size and much of the trail would be under water, but now the stream ran clear and low. As the bank on the South side rose to the rise of the foothills, Trey started Pepper across a shallow and gravel bottomed stretch of the stream. Followed closely by Praline, the horses took to the North side trail near the low creek banks.

"Since this is the first time out for our horses, we'll stop up here a ways at a little clearing and give them a break," said Trey over his shoulder to his companion.

"Sounds good to me, I think I could use a break too since this is my first time out since last fall. I need to stretch my legs out a little," replied Skye.

The break was short-lived but allowed the horses to get a few bites of grass and a long drink and the riders to break out some jerky and a long sip of cool water. Refreshed and back on the trail, both Trey and Skye settled into the easy rocking motion of the trail eating gait of their mounts. Trey breathed deeply as the trail rose above the stream and afforded a view of the valley below. It had been a gradual climb but the lower levels of the foothills of the Wind River Range still brought the slightly cooler breezes and what Trey believed to be much fresher air. Skye mimicked her friend and dropped the single rein to the neck of Praline, raised her arms to the blue overhead and said, "YES!"

Trey twisted in his saddle to turn back to see the cause for alarm, and with his right leg hooked over the cantle he said, "yes what?"

"Just yes. It is so good to be away from the school and everybody and out here in the wide open spaces. This is where we belong. Don't you agree?"

He smiled, shrugged his shoulders and chuckled as he turned back around in his saddle. To the North of the trail, the foothills rose with scattered large sandstone slabs and a broken mesa surrounded with a mantle of cliffs. Trey left the trail and rode his horse through a maze of sagebrush and creosote. Scattered clumps of wheatgrass and remnants of last summer's greenery tempted the horses to grab a bite on the move. The non-existent trail took them higher up the slope that led to an arroyo carved out by spring rainfalls of the past. Another quarter mile brought them to a scattering of large sharp cornered boulders that appeared to have broken from the mantle of cliff rock above them. Trey stopped his horse beside one of the larger boulders, stepped down and dropped his rein to ground tie Pepper. Skye joined him and held Praline's rein in her hand as she followed Trey's gaze to the overhead cliffs. High above the mesa, floating on the rising heat waves, a large golden eagle spread its wide wings as he dipped his head in his search for his next meal. Eagles were not a common sight and Trey and Skye both savored the moment as a sign of welcome.

The moment of silence was broken with the anxious question of Skye, "O.K. so where are they? I didn't come this far for nothing, did I?"grilled the grinning package of exuberance. Her dimple checked smile contradicted the firm manner of her question.

With a slow creeping grin spreading his face wide, Trey said quietly, "turn around."

She spun around and dropped to her knees drawing in a deep breath and whispered, "Oh my gosh! Look at that." Her eyes danced from figure to figure and she leaned one way and then another trying to get the right angle to see the figures and understand whatever story they sought to tell. Her arms stretched wide and she rocked back on her legs to drop to be seated on the ground. "Ohhh, ohh, wow."

She reached forward to touch but was stopped with a firm "Don't touch them," from Trey. She turned to look at him and her eyes held a question. "We can't damage them in any way. We shouldn't even touch them, especially with our bare hands. Anyway, before you get all wrapped up in these, let's get our horses settled in and then I've got some others for you to see."

They led their horses a short distance away from the stones to a more level spot with a little bit of last season's Brome grass, loosened the cinches and tethered the reins to a clump of sagebrush. Trey led the way up the small arroyo to an out thrust shoulder of stone, and climbing the escarpment he stopped at the crest of the shoulder and pointed to the cliff side. The dark brown patina of the cliff-face was decorated with the stone chipped or etched petroglyph figures highlighted by the exposed tan color of the carvings. With about 15 yards more climbing on all fours with hands digging in the loose dirt and grabbing anything for a handhold, feet sliding as toes dug in, and finally reaching the shelf of flat rock before the cliff face, they stood before the ancient graffiti like artwork rising far above their heads. Stepping back to the edge of the shelf for a

17

more panoramic view, Trey said, "Step back and look at the whole wall. Before you look at the small figures, you need to decipher the story, if there is one." Trey had seen this many times before and each time his appreciation of his elders and the ancients grew. It was easy for his imagination to take him back to some distant time and place him at this place carving these very figures. As Skye joined him and turned to look up at the figures, Trey asked, "Can you tell how they made those figures up at the top, those with the many animals?"

With a brief pause, a look up, and turning to Trey, she replied, "No. That's way too high for any man to reach. And it would be difficult to get a horse up here to stand on, but not impossible I guess. What do you think?"

"The answer is over there," he said as he pointed to the far left of the rock ledge, "see the figure in the corner?" She walked nearer the cliff-face and leaned to the side with an outstretched arm, then touched the image Trey indicated.

"A ladder? They made a ladder!" she exclaimed, returning to his side and again gazing at the many figures. "Do you know what those figures mean, what it says?"

He turned to her, looked to discern her sincerity, then with a slight step forward he lifted his hand pointing to the upper line of figures and said, "In the year of the bad summer and winter with very little snow, the shaman went to the great Spirit to plead for his people. Many had died, mostly old women and children, and the village was sad. The river was dry and fish were dead, and the deer and elk were few. The warriors had hunted but brought back very little game. He asked the Great Spirit for his help. Within 5 suns, the rains came and the village was saved. Animals returned, the river flowed again and fish returned. By the end of summer, the village was happy again and the Shaman thanked the Great Spirit."

Skye looked with wonder at Trey. For someone that had such difficulty reading in class, he showed amazing ability to interpret these ancient carvings and read them like a book. "How do you know that?" she asked, showing her amazement.

"See that first figure, with the straight line and circle below it? That means bad and the other line with the squiggles above it means bad summer. The arc with the circles and squiggles below it means winter, like falling snow. The figure of a man with the rays going from his head like sunlight means holy man or shaman. The diamond with circle in the middle means Great Spirit. Each figure has it's own meaning and it's like reading pictures." He turned at looked at Skye. "Of course, each one can read it to suit themselves, or what they want it to say, I suppose. You try reading this lower line. Tell me what it says."

She looked quizzically at the line indicated by Trey, thought a bit, and began, "The warrior went on his horse to hunt elk with his bow. The woman stayed at her lodge with the children. When the warrior returned he didn't have any game, so the woman beat him with a stick and made him go catch some fish for her and the children. When he returned, she cooked the fish, fed them to the children, ate some herself and made the man go hungry so he was sad. She went to the dance by herself and he stayed at the lodge with the children." Her mischievous smile spread while her eye gleamed with satisfaction as she looked at Trey.

"It doesn't say that!" he protested with a grimace.

"You said each one can read it to suit themselves. So, that suits me!" she declared with a broad grin.

"Maybe I should pray to the Great Spirit to bring down lightning to teach you a lesson on desecrating this land of the ancients!" he retorted, trying hard to maintain a somber expression, but failing as the grin stretched toward his ears.

Star Dancer

Chapter 4: Mustangs

SKYE TOOK LOTS OF PICTURES of the cliff-face with the many different carved figures as Trey sat with his feet hanging off the stone slab of shelf. Trey enjoyed surveying the vistas afforded by the lofty perch on the cliff wall with the snow-capped mountains of the Wind River range to his right and the lazy rolling plains stretching before him. He noticed a small dust cloud coming off the small hillock that dropped off to the North Fork in a point. The scattered pinion trees and sagebrush offered little shelter to any animal and Trey shielded his eyes in an effort to discern to cause of the dust. As his gaze lingered, whatever was making the dust was headed to the wide sandbar of the North Fork creek below him. As the dust cloud swirled, Trey began to see the small herd of mustangs clearly. They slowed to a trot and cautiously approached the stream, with the herd spread out. Numbering about a dozen, the mares and foals had eagerly crowded for a place to dip their noses in the refreshing stream. To the rear of the crowd, a tall and well muscled and scarred bay stallion tossed his head and watched over his herd. With his black mane waving like a flag of conquest, he brought a low whinney from deep in his chest that reverberated off the cliff behind Trey. Standing to get an even better look, he said to Skye. "Look Skye, mustangs!"

She turned and quickly stepped beside him, "Oh, I've never been this close before. Aren't they beautiful?"

He grinned as he responded, "Well, actually, they're a typically ragged looking bunch, but some of those foals look pretty good. Look at that dark sorrel at the far side over there. He acts like he's just waiting for his chance to challenge the big Bay. Now, he's a good looking horse. Look at his broad chest, and he's got some chrome, those two front stockings and blaze face, really everything about him looks good." Within moments, the big stallion pushed his herd across the stream and back uphill to quickly disappear beyond the arroyo. Trey stepped off the shelf and buried his heels in the loose soil to keep from slipping down the hill too fast. He extended his hand for Skye to steady her step but she jumped from the slight ledge and rapidly descended the hillside with large steps and digging her heels in to maintain her balance, "Come on, slowpoke. Whatcha waitin' on, Christmas?" she hollered over her shoulder to the surprised and stoic Trey. After a quick lunch of cold sandwiches and a face first drink from the stream, the two adventurers started the long trek back to civilization.

Sunday started as a lazy day. An impatient Tobey gently lifted a paw to the edge of Trey's bed, stretched a wet tongue to lick his face, and stepped back for his master to let him outside to do his business. Trey stumbled from his room to the back door and opened it wide for Tobey to make his quick exit. His bare chest felt the cool wind that heralded a Spring snow as he quickly shut the door and trotted back to his room to dive under the covers of his still warm bed. The pillow over his head did not muffle the call from his mother's room summoning him to her bedside. Before responding to her call, he slipped a t-shirt on and pulled it down over the top of his sweatpants, then padded into her room. His mom was sitting up in bed with a pillow behind her back and held a letter in her hand as she motioned to Trey to sit on the edge of the bed. "This letter came from the school yesterday and I just opened it this morning. We have to schedule a conference with your general education teacher, Mr. Whitson, sometime next week. With you being suspended and my work schedule, I think the best time would be either early Wednesday or Thursday. What do you think?" she asked as she looked at her son.

"I don't care, Mom. Whatever works for you. I have a free period at 10 every day."

"O.K., let's try for Wednesday. I'll call him tomorrow and set it up. Is there anything I need to be concerned about or prepared for with this conference?" she inquired.

"Not that I know of, I think it's just a regular conference like all the others."

"So, what are your plans for today? And the next two days, for that matter? You did a good job on the barn and your room, by the way. Thanks for that."

Trey and his mom had a good relationship and it was not unusual for them to have regular talks, nothing too long, but each had their own reservations and secrets. She was often complimentary and grateful for his helping hand with the chores around the house. Her work schedule made it difficult to spend much time together and with his dad gone with his work, planning any real family activities was not even considered. Trey had never been one for anything that involved crowds and noise, instead preferring time alone or with Skye. Both of them were happiest being outside, riding horses, and spending time together.

"Hadn't thought much about it. Skye and I saw some mustangs yesterday, I did think about maybe checking them out, see what they're up to, or maybe just go for a ride," he commented with a shrug of his shoulders.

"Well, Trey, you know I trust you. So, please, just be careful and if you're with Skye, take care of her and don't go doing anything that would get you into trouble. O.K.?"

"Sure mom, I won't," reassured Trey.

He made himself a couple of sandwiches from last night's pot roast, added a baggie of chips and grabbed an apple and an orange to top off his rations for the day. Putting his food in the saddle bags next to the packet of jerky, his binoculars and canteen in the opposite side, and taking a blanket and jacket, he went to the corral to finish his preparations for the day's excursion. As he mounted up, he whistled for Tobey and the dog came running excited about going with his master. Trotting alongside Pepper, Tobey yipped twice as he looked to Trey to show his approval. By the time the travelers made the first stop at the bank of the North Fork, both horse and dog wasted little time partaking of a long drink at the cool stream. With little snow-melt, the stream ran clear and low, but as the weather warmed, the increased melting snow would soon muddy the waters.

Early afternoon brought Trey to the mustang crossing of the North Fork. It was his plan to follow their trail and try to get an idea where he might find them. Before heading upstream on their trail, he stopped to have lunch and give the animals their due rest. As he sat down against the small cottonwood near the bank, Tobey lay at his side and sniffed for a handout. Trey dutifully shared a portion of his sandwich with him and scratched behind the dog's ears while Tobey looked to his master with his light blue eyes, expecting even more affection. Pepper lifted his head to see the two by the tree and joined in the family love fest by dropping his nose to Trey and sniffing the crumbs in his lap, then pushed his head to Trey's chest anticipating a good forehead rub and ear scratch. Trey did not disappoint his horse.

It was easy to follow the well-worn trail of the mustangs. For the first stretch, they followed the stream, then the trail followed the contour of the nearby hillside taking the mustangs over a saddle between two pinion covered hills and down to a open meadow of bluegrass and smaller patches of wheatgrass. The rising hills to the Northwest with the scattered juniper and pinion provided shelter from the cooler breezes coming from

24

the snow covered slopes of the Wind River range and Mount Wolverine specifically. As the trail topped the saddle, Trey brought Pepper to a stop by a nearby scrub Pinion. The lead mare of the small herd in the valley below lifted her head to determine if the disturbance on the ridge presented a threat. Frozen in place, without drawing a breath, she then lifted her nose to check the wind and any warning of danger. Satisfied, she dropped her head to continue her graze.

Trey slipped from his saddle, pushed Pepper behind the Pinion and tethered him to a low hanging branch, taking his binoculars from his saddlebags. Stepping to the side and dropping to one knee, Trey surveyed the herd. He was looking for the big sorrel stallion he admired the day before. He stood and turned to Pepper, then stepping around him, he made his way between the few trees and cactus to go to a higher spot on the hillside seeking to get a better view of the herd below. Tobey followed at his heels as the two found an inconspicuous assortment of large boulders partially obscured by more pinions. By climbing atop one of the smaller stones, Trey had a good view. Seating himself on one and leaning against another larger stone, Trey, with Tobey at his side, was able to start his vigil of the mustangs below.

Scanning the herd once, twice, with no sign of the sorrel, Trey started his scan again. A movement in the trees to the North of the herd caused him to swing his glasses to the trees. There was the sorrel, by himself, grazing but moving nervously. He would drop his head, grab some grass, lift his head and move around watching the herd. Trey didn't know if the sorrel was fearful for the herd or for himself, but the horse did appear skittish but cautious. Trey squirmed for a better seat on the hard rock, lifted his glasses again, and spoke to Tobey. "Boy, I don't know what he's doin' but he sure looks a bit scared. What is he doin'?" he asked Tobey as if he expected the dog to answer. Tobey raised his head, then sat up, whined his response, and stretched out again, content he had done his job.

On the opposite of the herd, the big bay stallion paraded back and forth, tossing his head, tail raised high and continually patrolled the perimeter of his herd. He too appeared somewhat nervous. Soon, the herd was moving more, milling about and watching their leader. Busting from the trees, the sorrel came charging to the edge of the herd, he held his head high with his mane flying across his back and his tail pointed skyward and trailing behind him. His stocking front feet pranced and lifted high in his stallion strut, showing off for the mares of the herd and attempting to intimidate the big bay stud. Raring up slightly, dropping his head, then charging to meet his challenger, the big bay let loose a squeal that trumpeted his dominance. He slid to a stop that stirred a dust cloud, he was obscured from view for a brief moment, then rising from the cloud with his front hooves pawing the air and his eyes full of fire, the bay determined to turn this adversary on his heels.

This was the first challenge mounted by the sorrel and he was not prepared for such a sudden and fierce attack by the big bay. Just that morning, the bay had nipped his hocks and driven him from the herd. It was a common practice for the herd stud to excommunicate any males coming of age that might threaten his dominance. Now, seeking re-admittance, he wasn't prepared to do battle with the big bay. He slid to a stop and started to rare up to meet the bay, but before he could lift his front feet, the bay brought his forefeet down on the neck and shoulders of the sorrel. The bay bared his teeth, laid his ears back and bit the withers of the smaller sorrel. Pulling away with a quick sidestep, the sorrel dropped his shoulders to loosen the bite, then spun to the side to make his escape. The bay chased him to the perimeter of the meadow and into the trees. Again raring up and squealing a warning, the bay then dropped to all fours and turned back to his herd. Without any significant injuries to anything but his pride, the sorrel disappeared into the trees that covered the hilltop to the North.

"Come'on Tobey, let's go see where that red horse went," called Trey to his furry companion. When Trey grabbed the reins, then swung atop Pepper, he was surprised when Tobey made a short leap from a large boulder behind the horse to land on the rump of Pepper. It was not unusual for the dog to hitch a ride with Trey and the sudden addition of another passenger did not surprise Pepper. They dropped below the shoulder of the hill and circled around to the Northwest to pick up the trail of the fleeing sorrel.

Following the trail for a couple of hours, it became evident the sorrel was circling around to the West and then the South of where the herd of mustangs had been grazing. Usually when a stallion is sent out on his own, he would try to gather his own herd of stragglers or other mares that were unattached. Other times they would return to try to subdue the herd stallion and take over their old herd. Trey was unable to discern the motivation of the sorrel based on the direction of his travel as he now passed the meadow of mustangs, he surmised the sorrel was headed to a specific location, either to other mustangs or a hide out to heal up and smarten up. With the sun now painting the Western sky from its palette of brilliance, Trey turned from his search and told Tobey, "It's time for us to head home, boy, dontcha think?"

Star Dancer

Chapter 5: Moonlight

THE RINGING OF THE PHONE rattled Trey awake. He rolled off the couch and went to the kitchen to grab the wall phone as it tried to vibrate itself off the wall with its incessant ringing. "Yeah!" he growled at the receiver as he stretched the cord to the table. Because of the intermittent cell reception on the reservation, most homes still had a land line for their primary phone service. A cheery voice questioned him from the other end, "Boy do you sound like a real grump. Whattsamatta, did I wake up the sleepyhead?" said Skye.

"No. Well, yeah, I just fell asleep on the couch. What are you doin' callin' me? Aren't you supposed to be in class?" he responded.

"No, the only class I had was Mrs. Watkins English and she cancelled because of some teacher's conference or something. So, I have the rest of the day off. Ya wanna go for a ride?"

"Sure, I guess. When? How soon?" he asked.

"I'll be there in about 15 minutes. O.K.?"

When Skye arrived, Trey had saddled Pepper, grabbed a few snack items from the fridge and cupboards, strapped on his saddlebags and a jacket and extra blanket and was just swinging aboard Pepper. Her little buckskin whinnied a greeting to her friend Pepper and Tobey ran circles around them both showing his excitement for another adventure. All were anxious to get to the hills so the two riders kicked their mounts to a canter. As they traveled, Skye quizzed Trey about his ride of the previous day and listened attentively to his story of the mustangs and the conflict between the two stallions.

"So, what do you think will happen to the sorrel now?" she asked.

"I don't know. I thought maybe we'd try to pick up his trail today and see where he went. Maybe he's looking for some other mares to make his own herd, or maybe he's just goin' to enjoy bein' on his own for a while. We'll see," replied Trey.

Arriving at the mustang crossing of North Fork, they dismounted and loosened the cinches on the saddles, let the horses get a good drink, then ground tied them by some graze. Trey carried his saddlebags to a spot of shade by a taller than average juniper and summoned Skye to join him. He shared some venison summer sausage and crackers for them to snack on while their horses had a breather.

"So, where exactly did you leave the trail of the sorrel?" inquired Skye as she stretched out and leaned back on one elbow, turning to look at Trey.

He sat cross-legged and assembled his sausage and cracker sandwich in anticipation of another snack. "Well, the herd was in a clearing by the creek about another 2 miles upstream. That's where he and the bay got into it, then he took off to the North but circled around, went over that big ridge to the South and up on top there is where I left his trail. I figger we'll stay on this side of the creek, and as we get a little farther up, we'll climb up on top and pick up his trail." "That's a pretty far stretch. If we go very far after that, it'll be well after dark when we get back. But, I guess that's all right, my Mom won't be gettin' home till late anyway." Skye's Mom and older sister worked at the tribal casino and her dad worked with Trey's dad in the oil field. The two considered each other as family since

30

their free time, which was often, was usually spent with one another, and they saw each other more than their own family members.

"Yeah, my Mom's workin' the late shift all this week at the restaurant, so I've got the time too. But, we'll get home before too late."

As they crossed the saddle at the top of the South ridge, they turned back to look down on the winding North Fork. Trey searched the creek bottom and remainder of the ravine for any sign of the mustang herd led by the big bay. With nothing indicating their presence, he turned Pepper back to the South and West to find the trail left by the sorrel. Vegetation was sparse on the mesa and they found the tracks of the sorrel just beyond where Trey had left the trail the day before. A two-track jeep road followed the contour of the flat top mesa to the West and it appeared the sorrel was also following the path of least resistance. Trey knew the road and knew it continued toward the tall timber of the Wind River mountains just to the West of the flat top mesa foothills. They followed the tracks as they cut across the jeep trail and turned back South to head up the side of the flat top mesa now on their left. Trey stopped, dismounted, and unstrapped his coat from behind the cantle of his saddle, Skye had donned her coat before they topped the ridge earlier. The higher elevation brought cooler air and the remaining snow on the North slopes together with the sun dropping behind the mountains, convinced Trey of the need of a coat.

Now properly attired in his oilskin wool lined duster with a split tail for his saddle, Trey felt every bit the mountain man. Though the sun was now behind the mountains, he pulled the brim of his hat down to look the part of the cowboy. Skye watched him and knew what he was thinking, for he often voiced his wish of turning back time to the "old days" but he often waffled between the traditional Arapaho ways and the ways of the old cowboys. She stifled a chuckle and kneed her buckskin as not to be left behind.

"If we don't spot him pretty soon, it'll be too dark to follow his tracks. We'll have to try again another day," he surmised.

"Yeah, like you need another excuse to come back up here. Course, I guess you do have another day on that suspension. But, if you come back tomorrow, I can't come with you. One of us doesn't get into trouble and get kicked out of school. I wonder who that is?" she kidded.

The trail meandered across the mesa from one patch of grass to another, although the bits of grass were sparse, some were starting to show a little green as a result of the early Spring snow melt. The general direction of the trail was back to the East across the top of the mesa. Soon, they dropped off the shoulder and through a few scrub pinion. Darkness had caught them as they dropped to the bottom of the draw and came upon another jeep road. "I know this road, it goes back to Ft. Washakie, probably best we just follow it out. The full moon will give us plenty of light, but it will be easier goin' for the horses." The trail of the sorrel had crossed the road and appeared to go to the trees on the side of the smaller mesa to the East of the road. The edge of the full moon was just peeking above the mesa and illumined the road before them. Overhead the blackness of the night was being decorated with the many stars racing to be the first to show their brilliance. The beauty of the night brought a stillness to the creation around them and they lifted their eyes to enjoy the display seldom seen by the city dwellers in their concrete jungles with artificial lights and man-made noise. The muffled hoof steps of the two mounts were the only reminders of life when Skye lifted her hands to trace the path of the Milky Way across the night sky. As she followed the light of the magnificent constellation, her hand dropped to the blackness of the Eastern horizon atop the Mesa, something else caught her eye.

"Trey, look," she said as she pointed to the edge of the black Mesa and reined her horse to a stop. "There!"

Trey turned first to Skye, and following her pointing, he turned to look to the edge of the black mesa. Illumined by the full moon, a silhouetted horse reared up and pawed the night sky with his front hooves. With his long mane trailing down his neck to his back, he appeared to be playing a musical tune on the stars as a pianist would the keys of his instrument. He dropped to all fours, reared again, and continued his dramatic presentation of magnificence and beauty. Both Trey and Skye were mesmerized and wordlessly watched the spectacle. A sight seldom seen, the lone stallion repeated his performance, dropped again to all fours and pranced beyond sight across the top of the dark mesa.

Trey whispered, "It was like he was dancing on the stars," then turning to Skye, "wasn't he beautiful? That had to be the sorrel. It was too dark to see his color, but I'm sure it was him. Don't you think so?" he asked Skye, seeking reassurance for his comment.

"I'm sure it was. He was beautiful, wasn't he?" she said as she reminded him they needed to be getting back home.

Star Dancer

Chapter 6: Wounded

TUESDAY WAS THE LAST DAY of the suspension. Trey wanted to take advantage of the full day to find the Sorrel, to what end he didn't know, but he felt compelled to find him. He told his Mom last night about his plans and she reluctantly agreed. She well knew his love of horses and his infatuation with the mustangs and had reconciled his obsession as better than the many other things that teenagers used to destroy their lives. Her work schedule seemed to consume her every free moment and thought, and as long as Trey was not into anything dangerous or destructive, she considered her parental efforts a success. Now Trey was getting an early start on his quest to find the source of his sleepless nights and anxious days.

Trey really didn't know what he expected, but he wanted to be prepared. Besides taking enough food and snacks for the day, he also packed his rope, two piggin' strings (The short small ropes used by ropers to tie the legs of calves after roping), and a rope halter with lead. His day dreams had him capturing the Sorrel and making him some great horse, of course he didn't know how he was going to accomplish this great dream, but he wanted to be ready for the opportunity. With a whistle for Tobey, he mounted up and pointed Pepper to the familiar mountains. Two hours brought them to the shallow crossing of the North Fork and after wading the shallow stream, the traveling trio stopped in the shade of the cottonwoods for a break and a snack.

Trey tossed a morsel of jerky in the air above Tobey's head and watched him jump to retrieve it. Pepper busied himself with some of the fresh sprouts of grass at the bank of the stream. As was often the case, Trey carried on a one sided conversation with his dog. "So, Tobey, where do you think we'll find the Sorrel today? I'm thinkin' we'll check out the small pasture where the herd was the other day, maybe they're back and the Sorrel might be hangin' around too." Tobey, sitting on his haunches, cocked his head to the side at his master with a questioning expression on his face. "I know, neither one of us really knows where he'll be, but we gotta start somewhere, don't we?" he said as he stood up and Tobey ran around him as a sign of agreement with whatever his master said, as long as he was included, Tobey really didn't care.

Following his trail of the previous pursuit of the herd, another hour had passed before they reached the crest of the hill overlooking the small meadow. Cautiously Trey pointed his mount to the taller of the junipers that lined the crest of the hill so as to obscure himself from the view of anything down below. Dismounting and giving the rein a quick wrap around a sizable branch, with binoculars in hand and Tobey by his side, Trey worked his way to the boulders that made his converted couch on the previous trip. Tobey beat him to the boulder and stretched out on the foremost edge, while Trey seated himself with his back to the smooth side of the topmost stone. An extended squeal from below caught his attention and as he looked down, the herd was milling around but all were watching an ongoing battle between two magnificent stallions.

Looking like two prizefighters in a boxing ring, the two stallions were reared on hind legs and sparring with their front hooves. The big bay stood taller and with his teeth bared and ears laid back, he sought to bite the sorrel by reaching for his neck then his withers, each time biting to get a grip to disable his challenger. With his fore hooves striking at the blaze face of the sorrel, the big bay launched himself at the red horse and barreled him over with his superior weight. The sorrel kicked with all fours to push himself out of reach of the bay, and with a glancing blow of his hind foot struck the bay beside his nostrils causing him to side step out of the way of the deadly hind legs. The white stocking front feet of the sorrel pushed at the loose soil as he regained his feet. Laying his ears back and with his long mane flying over his withers, the sorrel charged at the side of the bay using his broad chest as a battering ram, he succeeded in downing the bay. His teeth locked on the bay's neck and he drew blood, but the strength of the big bay had not waned and he rose to his feet and jerked his neck free from the sorrel's teeth. He whirled around and kicked at the sorrel with both hind legs and landed a glancing blow to the right shoulder with his ragged hooves tearing a gash between the withers and the shoulder.

Trey was breathless as he watched the battle below. It was evident by the turned up soil and the lathered combatants that the contest had already been lengthy. Both stallions were blooded in several places and they were slower in their responding charges toward one another. Trey wanted his sorrel to be the champion but he was more concerned about his survival. He whispered to his sorrel, "Just get away, he's going to kill you. Run!"

As if he heard the plea, the sorrel turned away from the bay, but the bay sought an advantage and pursued. With wide eyes showing white, the bay stretched his head with his teeth bared, pulled partially alongside the sorrel and again gave a vicious bite at the base of the neck of the sorrel. The sorrel kicked back with his hind leg and landed a solid blow to the ribs of the bay that caused him to drop away. With this reprieve, the red horse stretched out and made his escape through the trees. "YES! Run boy run!" shouted Trey, startling Tobey.

He ran back to Pepper and quickly drew the rein from the branch, and without using the stirrup he threw a leg over his mount and whistled to Tobey. The dog jumped as high as he could to Trey, was caught, and set behind his master on the rump of Pepper. Trey kneed Pepper and started down the slope toward the herd. Passing behind the gathered mares, the herd was startled and as one scattered to the North side of the meadow and the nearby trees. Trey slowed his mount as they entered the scattered junipers and pinions searching for the trail of the sorrel. He quickly spotted the fresh tracks of the fleeing stallion and set his course to follow the trail.

The deep and stretched out tracks soon changed to closer paced and no longer dug into the soil. The stallion had slowed and now had irregular steps and sometimes swayed from one side of the trail to the other. It was easy to see the horse was tired and wounded and occasional spots of blood showed on the trail. Nearing a narrow ravine that was fronted by some large boulders, Trey was surprised to see shoulder high blood on the larger boulder beside the trail. It was unusual for a horse to lean against anything and the blood on the boulder revealed much about the severity of the wounds of the big sorrel. His tracks turned up the ravine surprising Trey, but then he remembered there was a small spring at the head of this narrow draw. The large boulders stacked at the entrance appeared like the pillars at the entrance of an ancient palace. With several small twisted cedars digging their roots into the crevices between the individual stones to cling tenuously to life and stretch their gnarled limbs skyward with the green sprigs sheltering the dusty blue berries below.

Trey dropped to the ground, dropped one rein and placed a large stone on top to remind Pepper he was ground tied. Toby awaited Trey with the stub of his tail wagging a "hurry up" to his master. Trey slowly rounded the crook formed by the out-thrust of a stone wall as he followed the sandy bottom trail into the ravine. Less than 100 yards further up the draw, a small grove of aspen surrounded the spring and grassy knoll where the big sorrel was stretched on his side. He didn't move as Trey silently approached. Not wanting to scare the stallion, Trey swung wide to the shady side of the ravine, and climbed the bank a few steps to get a better view of the prone red horse. Trey squatted on his heels, and dropped a hand to Tobey to quiet the dog. As he watched the sorrel, he could see his side slowly rise and fall, then with a quick survey he also noted several bloody wounds, some apparently still bleeding. There was drying lather between his hind legs, below his flanks, behind his front legs on his chest and by his throat latch. It was evident the horse was not just badly wounded but exhausted as well. Trey slowly rose, snapped his fingers to Tobey, and quietly exited the ravine.

As he stood beside Pepper, he looked at the entrance to the ravine and thought, *I've got to do something so he won't leave here. I need time to go home and get the medicine he needs, but I can't let him get away. Maybe if I use my rope and . . .* he looked around for anything else that would help make a fence to cover the entrance to the ravine. Reaching behind the cantle of his saddle to a scabbard that was pretty much a permanent fixture, he withdrew the combination bone/wood saw. The scabbard held a skinning knife and the saw, which was about 14 inches long and serrated on both sides. One side was for cutting wood while the other side had closer spaced and smaller teeth for cutting bone. The aluminum handle was hollow and contained matches. This was a survival kit that Trey had always carried at the instruction of his father. Now i was going to help the survival of a big red horse. Trey wasted little time cutting and fetching the lower and longer limbs of the nearby juniper trees, each measuring about five feet long.

Dropping the loop of his rope around a five foot boulder, he then stretched it across the ravine at a height of about six feet, then secured it to a larger cedar well entrenched in the widening crack of a larger boulder. He used the piggin strings from his saddle bags and with short cut pieces, secured the branches to the rope, giving the appearance of an impenetrable barrier. Trey knew if the horse wasn't wounded, he would make short work of his fence, but he still hoped this would at least secure him till he returned. He then mounted up, whistled to Tobey, and started on what he hoped would be a quick round trip.

As he tethered his horse to the post by the house, he reviewed the list he had made in his mind on the return trip. He ran around back to the tack shed and began rummaging in the one cabinet for his supplies. *Bag balm, yeah, elastic wrap, yeah, gauze pads, yeah, bute? Ace? Maybe in the house. More rope, twine, squirt bottle with disinfectant, yeah.* With his arms full of his supplies, he headed to the back door and into the kitchen. Looking in the fridge for some ace (an injection used to calm or sedate) he found only one syringe with an out of date label. He grabbed the phone and dialed Skye's number while he searched the drawers for a tube of bute (an anti-inflammatory and pain medication). All of these supplies are common in most rural households that have large animals and it wasn't unusual for Trey to use them on his and his grandmother's horses. The phone now rang for the fourth time.

"Hello" said Skye, out of breath from running to answer the phone.

"Skye, I need some Ace and some Bute, ya got any?" asked Trey anxiously.

"Uh, yeah, I think so. What's the matter? Is Pepper hurt?"

"No, it's for the sorrel. He and the big bay had a whale of a fight and the sorrel got the worst of it. He needs some doctoring right away" he explained.

"The sorrel? How ya gonna doctor him? He's wild!" she asked.

"I don't have time to explain, can you bring that stuff over?"

"Sure. But I'm coming with you!" she stated and hung up the phone before Trey could argue.

Chapter 7: Doctoring

TETHERING THEIR HORSES to a large juniper near the entrance to the ravine, they loosened the cinches on the saddles and grabbed the saddle bags with the assorted supplies needed. Climbing the large boulders that guarded the entrance, the two would be vets made a trail on the high side of the North bank of the ravine. "So, how we gonna do this? You know we've got to get some Ace in him before we'll be able to do much" observed Skye.

"I know," Trey said as he led the way to the head of the ravine, "I figger I'll let you come up on him from down below while I make my way through the quakies and see if I can get a dose in his rump before he spooks."

"Oh, so you want me to be out in front of this wild stallion that's madder than an ole hornet, while you sneak up on him from the safety of the trees. That's big of you" she remarked.

"Well, would you rather do the sneakin'?"

"Yeah, I would. At least that way, if he spooks, he'll be chargin' at you and not me!"

With their plan set, Skye began her trek to the head of the ravine, doing her best to stay out of sight. While he waited, Trey sorted the supplies and made ready with the rope halter and the additional lariat. He would leave the supplies by the rock ledge before making his way to the bottom of the ravine. The plan was for him to slowly approach within full view of the stallion to keep his attention away from the approach of Skye through the quakies. When he spotted her approach to the upper edge of the trees, he slid to the bottom of the slope and started up the ravine. He walked slowly, avoiding eye contact, and spoke very softly just low enough to keep the attention of the stallion. As he neared the trees, the horse slowly lifted his head to view this new threat. As he watched the approach of Trey, the stallion struggled to rise to his feet, but as he got his front hooves out in front of him and stretched his neck in an effort to get his hind legs under him, Skye quickly drove the needle of the syringe into his rump and plunged the syringe to empty the Ace into the stallion. The red horse swung his head back to see this new threat to watch Skye retreat into the trees. Swinging his head back to watch the first threat, he observed Trey backing away to take up a vigil in the rocks.

"Whooaa, that was a rush!" exclaimed Skye as she dropped down beside Trey.

"We're lucky he was so tired and sore. We could never do that if he wasn't."

"Well, in about 10 minutes, he should be in LaLa land, and we can get to doctoring those wounds. I noticed a couple on his neck and withers," said Skye," but I think the worst ones are on this side."

As the two began their dressing of the wounds, Skye started with the spray bottle filled with the diluted Betadine as an antiseptic, and did her best to clean the open wounds. Trey used the Bute paste injector and gave a measured dose of Bute under the tongue of the stallion. The Bute would help with the pain and inflammation of the wounds. Two larger wounds concerned Trey, one a large laceration at the point of the shoulder just below the withers, and the other an extended cut along the right front cannon bone. After spray cleaning the other wounds, Skye dressed them with copious amounts of Bag

Balm to keep out any dust and hasten the healing and scarring of the cuts. Pointing to the two larger wounds, Trey said, "These two are going to need bandages." Then pointing at the larger wound on the shoulder, he said, "You spray it, and I'll shave some of that hair so the tape will stick."

"That bandage won't stay on too long," stated Skye, "without being able to wrap it around something."

"That's why I'm going to shave off some hair, so the bandage can stick to the skin."

Trey used his skinning knife to shave off as much hair as he could, then with a large gauze pad with bag balm on it, the slapped the pad on the wound, barely covering it. Using the only tape he had, good old duct tape, he pressed the tape to the bare skin and pushed it as tight as he could. Then he turned his attention to the still bleeding wound on the leg. Skye had sprayed it and prepared a couple of gauze pads for him. Taking the roll of blue elastic wrap, he applied the pads to the wound and wrapped the leg repeatedly to secure the pads tightly to the wound. Although their doctoring efforts had taken almost thirty minutes, it seemed to be just a few and both were surprised as the stallion started to stir and tried to lift his head. They quickly grabbed the rest of their supplies and stepped away from the stirring and groggy stallion.

Many of the injuries to the red horse were not open wounds but bruises and scrapes, perhaps a cracked rib or two, but no other obvious injuries were noted by the concerned duo. They followed the same trail out of the ravine as they returned to their mounts to secure the saddlebags and supplies. Trey had brought an additional rope and twine to reinforce the barrier at the opening and now proceeded with the task. Trey stretched the new rope across the opening and secured it in similar fashion as the first rope, Skye followed along, using the twine to secure the branches to the additional rope and use other branches to fill in any obvious openings.

"Well, it ain't the purtiest fence I ever saw, but I think it'll hold him. At least until he gets better and decides he wants out. Then, I don't know . . . " observed Skye.

As the two tightened the cinches on their saddles and mounted up, Skye asked, "So, now what? What are you gonna do with him?"

"You mean the stallion?" Trey replied, "I'm not sure. I think I'd like to break him, train him. I think he'd make a fantastic mount. As beautiful as he is, I think he could father some mighty fine foals."

"You say, train him. For what? Team roping, barrels, reining, cutting, anything special?"

"Kind of all around. For competition I think they call it versatility, or something like that. They have to do it all, cutting, roping, obstacle course, all of it. I saw a competition last summer in Riverton. It was pretty special," answered Trey.

They were riding down the same jeep trail they had followed the night they saw the stallion on the horizon above them. Dusk was just starting to fall and they watched a pair of mule deer doe scamper across the trail and up into the trees on the slope beside them. Skye kneed her buckskin up beside Trey and Pepper, and said, "But you've never trained a horse like that before, have you?"

"No, but I think with your help, we can get it done. What I don't know, you do. And what you don't know, we'll just have to figger it out!" he said conclusively. "I'm gonna come back up here every day if I can. Then on the weekends and after school is out in about a month, we'll have every day we can work with him. By that time he'll be comfortable with us and we can start doing some serious training. Don't ya think?"

Skye just looked at him. She wondered about him, often having difficulty in school but not afraid to try anything else. Things that would cause most people to step back or even give up, he would figure things out, solve the problem and finish whatever he started. She shook her head and said, "I suppose anything's possible. Especially as stubborn as you are."

Chapter 8: Conference

TREY'S MOM, SOPHIE, wasn't used to getting out and about in the middle of the morning. With her late schedule, her days usually didn't start until early afternoon, but today was an exception. The scheduled conference with Trey's general education teacher seemed to be a little more important than previous conferences, based on the emphasis of the teacher for her attendance. Trey was already seated when his mom entered the conference room, an office borrowed from the guidance counselor. The teacher, Mr. Whitson, rose from his chair as she entered and he motioned her to a chair beside Trey and immediately in front of the desk.

"Good morning. I'm happy to see you. Go ahead and have a seat and we'll get started," he stated as he seated himself. He shuffled a few papers together, stood them on end and tapped them to align them and set the stack down to his left, leaving the top of the desk free of clutter. He clasped his hands together and began, "Mrs. StandingElk, as we near the end of the school year and Trey's first year in the high school, I'm concerned about the progress, or lack of it, of Trey. He seems to be struggling quite a bit, especially in the language courses."

45

Sophie interjected, "Are you talking about his behavior in class?" as she wrinkled her brow with the question.

"No, no. It's not that, although he has had some recent difficulties. What I'm concerned about is his learning. Let me explain." He leaned back and took a deep breath as if trying to gather his thoughts. Sophie watched him carefully and waited, all the while wondering what exactly he was trying to explain.

"At the half way point in the school year, I give an in-depth evaluation to all my students. As you know, I'm the general education teacher for Trey, but he has several other teachers for the different classes. After I look at the records, if necessary I confer with any teachers directly involved in any problem areas. We then try to chart a course that would make his learning experience most beneficial," he stated as he nodded toward Trey. He continued, "If there is enough concern, we refer the program to the BIT or the Building Intervention Team, to design an appropriate program or intervention to ensure Trey is progressing properly. During this last half of the year, we have instituted several different things from the Mentor program, the Team program and an introduction to the Tutor program. Regrettably, these programs have not accomplished what we hoped. So, now what I would like to recommend is a comprehensive special education evaluation to see if Trey might have a disability. To do that we will need the written permission of the parents."

Sophie dropped her head and looked at her hands in her lap. She remembered a conference like this when Trey was in elementary school, and as she thought back on that time, the emotions began to parade through her mind and heart like a marching band on parade with emphasis on the big and loud bass drum that beat the constant cadence now banging in her head. She clenched her teeth and brought her hands into tight fists as she sought to control herself and gather her thoughts. She knew her son had struggled with reading and speaking in front of people, and that he wasn't comfortable with crowds, but that didn't make him disabled! She knew he was intelligent

46

because she knew of the many times he had been confronted with problems and had found solutions that were beyond her abilities. She felt there wasn't anything her son couldn't do or learn, it just might take him time or he might have to reach the answer in a different way, but he wasn't disabled. Taking a deep breath, she lifted her head to address the teacher.

"Mr. Whitson, I know my son is not disabled. I also know that if I suggested to his father that he needs evaluation to see if he's disabled, his father would go through the roof like a moon rocket. He would never consent to anyone even implying that his son was disabled. It just won't happen. Now the way I understand it is, the basis of all learning is his ability to read, am I right?"

"Well, simply put, yes. But that's where he seems to have the greatest difficulty," he pleaded.

"No, he is quite capable of reading. Yes, there are times he might struggle with certain words or similar words, but I think the problem is not with the reading so much as it is with reading aloud in front of the class," she summarized. "So, since his father certainly won't allow this evaluation, is there any other alternative that we might pursue to help my son?"

"I'm really not sure, Mrs. StandingElk. To be honest with you, I think your son may be dyslexic. That can manifest itself in many different ways including in his reading. It's not really a visual problem as a way that the brain processes the information. Different people have different difficulties but it's not something to be ashamed of, but rather a challenge to overcome. Now, if that was the problem, and I'm not saying it is, but if it is then what would happen is he would be given a special curriculum and instruction. But since that can't happen, maybe if you had a tutor, someone with experience with dyslexia, maybe that would give Trey the tools to work with and meet this challenge."

"Mr. Whitson, when Trey was in elementary school, his teacher swore up and down that Trey had ADHD and that he needed medication. I thought then and I still believe it today, that the teacher just couldn't handle the challenge of an active boy. But we went to the doctor and got the prescription, and all it did was practically make Trey into a Zombie. He was listless and slept all the time, but he sure didn't act up in class. He couldn't because he was usually sleeping. After about a month of that, we took him off and he hasn't had it since, but he has managed to make it this far in school. I know my son is intelligent and I definitely don't believe he's disabled, but I will check it out and see if there is anything we can do." She rose from her seat and turned to leave, "Thank you, Mr. Whitson. I know you're just concerned and I appreciate your concern. Trey, walk me to the car please."

As they walked to the parking lot, Sophie turned to her son. "Trey, don't let this get you down. One person's opinion doesn't shape you, the only thing that matters is your own opinion of yourself. Don't ever forget, you are a fantastic young man and you are not disabled. If you have any difficulty with anything, together we can find a solution. Remember that. O.K.?"

"Sure Mom. I appreciate you standing up for me in there. Mr. Whitson is all right, but there's a couple others that just don't have any patience and if you're not like all the others, they want to either change you or get rid of you," he stated. It was the first time he had ever shared his opinion about any of his teachers and she looked at him to see if there was more. He dropped his head and said, "I've got other things goin' on anyway. School will be out soon and we can take a better look at things then. Have a good day at work, O.K.?" He then turned to go back to his next class.

The rest of the school day went like every other day, bells rang, classes changed, kids yelling in the halls, and teachers trying to instill knowledge to resistant students. Trey took advantage of every opportunity to day dream while gazing at the distant mountains, and thought of the big red stallion. He began to make mental notes of all that would be necessary to start the training. First he had to concern himself with food and water. The water was all right from the spring, but he might have to dig out a small pool to make it easier to drink. Then he needed to provide some food. The grass by the spring wouldn't be enough to last very long and once it was grazed down, it might not come back. He thought he might take some grain and maybe even some hay up to him. His day dreaming helped to pass the time and shortly the bell rang to signal the end of his school day. Without hesitation he hurried to his locker, stashed his books, grabbed his bag and headed home. He might have time to make it up to see the sorrel if he hurried.

Star Dancer

Chapter 9: Friends

NOTHING HAD CHANGED. The barrier at the entrance of the ravine held fast, there was no sign of any effort on the part of the stallion to make an escape. Tying off Pepper at the usual juniper, Trey pulled his warbag from behind the cantle of his saddle. He had filled it with some grain, a collapsible shovel, a black rubber feed pan, and topped it off with several flakes of grass hay. Putting the strap over his shoulder, he mounted the boulders to make his way to check on the stallion. The sides of the ravine were steep and rocky with occasional scrub pinion trees clinging to any patch of dirt near projecting stones while scattered clusters of prickly pear cactus added obstacles to anything attempting to mount the steep banks. Several large outcroppings of stone extended themselves over portions of the cutaway banks to provide shelter to any vagabond creature below. It was under the largest of these overhangs that Trey began to set up his shelter and storage.

Carrying his shovel, Trey walked to the head of the ravine to find the stallion standing at the same place where they bandaged his wounds. The horse turned his head toward Trey, ears forward, eyes attentive. Although standing with his side toward the intruder, the red horse did not move. Trey noted both bandages still intact, and no evidence of any additional bleeding. Red horse was standing three legged with his left back hock bent and his hoof toed into the ground. The only movement was a slight muscle twitch from his right front forearm to his shoulder at the bandaged wound. His eyes were bright and he watched Trey with curiosity. Standing by the grove of aspen, the spring was in front of him and slightly below the bit of rise where he waited.

Trey began to speak softly and walked at an angle toward the spring, carefully watching the stallion from the corner of his eye. He knew that any wild animal would watch the eye of any perceived threat and that direct eye contact usually indicated a prey and predator. Continuing to speak and walking slowly, he approached the spring. Stepping across the trickle of water that emerged from below a stack of rocks, he determined a place to make a pool for the water and began to shovel it out. The spring ran slowly but consistently and with a deep enough pool, the horse would have ample drinking water. Completing his task, Trey bent with cupped hands to afford himself a refreshing drink from the spring. All the while, the red horse watched and did not move, never feeling threatened.

Leaving the spring, Trey returned to the overhang shelter, dropped the shovel and picked at his warbag. He withdrew the flakes of hay, sat one aside, and stacked the rest on a shelf at the back of the overhang, then stacked a series of rocks in front of them to prevent the red horse having an uninvited feeding. He took the feed pan and put the bulk of the grain in it and placed it with the extra hay. With the flake of hay under one arm and a large handful of grain in his other hand, Trey made his way back towards the aspen grove. Again walking at an angle in the direction of the spring, Trey stopped at the edge of the grassy knoll, dropped the hay, put the grain in a small pile on top of the flake, then taking a small bag of powdered Bute from his pocket, he sprinkled the hay around the grain with the powder. He rose and carefully and slowly made his retreat.

Now he would watch, watch and wait. Stepping away from the spring about 20 yards, he scratched his way on all fours up the side of the bank to a sizable stone. Seating himself on the stone, he bent one knee, clasped his hands around it and waited. The red horse watched. Trey did not move, and after about a quarter of an hour, the stallion took a tentative step toward the spring. With each step, he would turn his head and look at Trey. Another step, another turn of his head. Then two steps, and three, and as he reached the spring, he looked again at Trey, then dropped his head and took a long drink from the small pool of fresh spring water. Lifting his head and looking again at his adversary, the red horse then turned to face Trey. His curiosity now prompted him to slowly step to the small pile left by the man. As he neared the hay, he again looked at Trey and certain he hadn't moved, he then dropped his muzzle to sniff the offering. With his head down, he still eyed Trey, then curled his lip and tasted the grain. This was undoubtedly a new treat to the wild mustang, but apparently a pleasing one as he dropped his head to continue his meal. Take a bite, raise his head and look at Trey, take a bite and repeat.

The sorrel's supper had taken about a half an hour, and during that time of scrutiny, Trey never moved. He watched and made eye contact with the stallion and neither spooked. As the sorrel finished the hay, picking up the few scattered pieces, he stopped and looked at Trey. The boy was seated on a large stone that put his seat at about the same height as the shoulder of the stallion and necessitated the horse to raise his head to look directly at Trey's face. With no movement from the boy, the horse took one then two steps toward the stone and its occupant. He stopped, snorted, bobbed his head up and down, then took another step. With no other movement from Trey, the red horse tossed his head high, whirled on his back right foot, and returned to his comfortable corner of the ravine by the aspen grove. He then turned to see if he had been followed and watched as Trey slid down the side of ravine and made his way down to the shelter overhang.

Trey grabbed his now empty warbag, threw it over his shoulder and climbed the boulders to exit the ravine. With a quick check of the rope and branch barrier, he picked up Pepper's rein, lifted his foot to the stirrup and mounted. He turned around in the saddle, strapped his warbag down, and with a whoop he dug his heels into Pepper and leaned forward over his neck to lope away from the ravine. Again he dug his heels into Pepper's ribs, and let out another long whoop as they galloped through the fast falling dusk along the jeep trail towards home. Trey was overflowing with excitement and joy as he thought of the progress he made with the stallion. Now reining Pepper back, he relived the moments before, knowing he had made friends with the red horse. Many would think nothing had been accomplished, but Trey knew that trust had emerged. The stallion had actually approached in his direction, not as a threat but out of curiosity and that curiosity had bred trust. He knew that as trust was built, and then dependence on Trey for food and care, that a bond of friendship would be the foundation for training.

Friends. He had made friends with a mustang. And not just any mustang, but the red stallion. Now passing the hillside where they had first seen the sorrel silhouetted against the night sky, Trey remembered how he seemed to be dancing on the stars. *That's it! That's what his name will be, Star Dancer!* With another whoop that startled Pepper, he kicked his mount to a trot, anxious to talk to Skye about Star Dancer.

Chapter 10: Conspirators

DARKNESS HAD DROPPED her skirts by the time Trey walked his horse, Pepper, up the long dirt road to his house. Without the bright street lights of the city and the headlights of traffic, it was easy for his eyes to adjust to the deepening darkness. With the sliver of the new moon and a sky full of stars, Trey rocked his hips with the steady gait of his horse and contemplated his experience with Star Dancer. His father, Stoney, had spent his youth on a nearby ranch and many summers were occupied with breaking colts and training them for the ranch work. As a boy, Trey had watched many of his neighbors breaking the yearlings the same way his father had done on the ranch. As his father often said, "It's simple, ya ketch 'em, saddle 'em, break 'em, and use 'em." But Trey knew there were better ways, and he was determined not to break the spirit of Star Dancer, but become one with him and together they could do anything.

Just the expression of breaking a horse, did not sit easy with Trey. He could see the difference in a foal full of life and excitement and spirit and then after breaking, the light in his eyes was gone and the spirit was indeed broken. He didn't want that for Star Dancer and he was determined to do it different,

Star Dancer

he wasn't sure how, but he would find a way. He looked toward his house and could see a horse tethered at the post by the side of the home and it appeared that someone was sitting on his doorstep.

Skye hailed him as he approached, "Hey Trey. About time, I was beginning to think that stallion and kicked your skull in and I was goin' to have to go pick up the pieces."

"Not hardly, but you shoulda been there. Come on around back while I put Pepper up and I'll tell ya all about it."

Trey stepped down from his saddle and with a loose hanging rein with Pepper following, he walked beside Skye to the backyard corral. With practiced movement, he slipped the saddle and bridle from his horse, turned him into the corral and took his gear to the tack shed. As he returned, he joined Skye at the pole fence and put a foot on the bottom rail and leaned with both arms on the top. Skye had already seated herself on the top rail and now looked down at Trey and said, "O.K., tell me about it. I've been waiting here forever just to hear this tall tale of yours, so out with it."

Beginning with his approach with the shovel and the digging out of the spring, he finished with his galloping departure aboard Pepper and his revelation at the new name for the stallion.

"Star Dancer. I like it! It sure fits him, cuz that's what he was doing when we saw him up on that mesa. He sure was beautiful. So, how's all his injuries doin'? Are the bandages still holdin'?" asked Skye.

"Yeah, both the bandages were lookin' good, and so were all the other scrapes you doctored. You did a good job. And the way he was actin' I don't think he'll be lazin' around much. You could still tell he had some soreness and swelling in places, but he looks good. I put some powdered Bute in with the grain and hay and he made short work of it, so I think he'll heal up real good."

"Are you still set on doin' that versatility training?" inquired Skye.

56

"I don't know. One time it's versatility, then next time I think about it, it's somethin' else. I think we'll just have to take our time and see what's right for him," drawled Trey. "You know, how he responds to whatever we try to teach him."

"I think that's smart. Like my daddy used to say, you need to train a horse to match his personality, and if you do it right, the horse will train you to do what he's best at. So, by the way, how did your teacher conference go this morning?"

He cocked his head to look up at her, then back down as he dropped one hand to his knee. "Not so good. Mr. Whitson tried to talk Mom into having me evaluated for special education. He says he thinks I might be Dyslexic. Just because I'm not real good at reading, he thinks I'm messed up," he growled. "Then he suggested I get a special tutor or some kinda help like that, and my Mom almost hit the ceiling, cuz my Dad would definitely come unglued about that and we can't afford any special tutor." Trey hit his fist on the top rail so hard it vibrated under Skye.

"Dang, Trey. Whatcha gonna do?" replied Skye.

"I don't know. Part of me says I just oughta quit school and forget about it . . . "

"You don't wanna do that. It's hard enough to get a job as it is, but with no education, it's a lost cause. Don't quit, whatever you do, don't quit," she pleaded. A whimper from his feet caused Trey to look down into the blue eyes of his Australian Shepherd, Tobey, who was anxious to welcome his master home. Trey dropped a hand to scratch him behind his ears and ruffle the fur on his chest, then he turned back to Skye.

"I said a part of me wants to quit, but the rest of me says, fight it out. I know I'm not dumb, but it does take a while for me to make sense out of anything I try to read," he stated as he helped her down from her perch on the fence. They walked side by side back to the front doorstep and sat down together. "Mom said she'd see what we can do, but I don't know what she can do. Back in elementary school when the teacher thought I had ADHD, we tried the tutor route and that didn't help, but when I took my time and concentrated, I was able to figure out most of it and I made it this far, so I guess we'll just wait and see what happens."

Thursday and Friday saw the routine of Wednesday repeated. Each day, Trey left school as early as possible and headed to the mountain as fast as Pepper could go, while Tobey would race along at his heels. He established a pattern with Star of bringing a flake of hay, a little grain, some powdered Bute and then stepping away to watch from his perch on the big boulder. Tobey would wait patiently while seated on the boulder and would usually drop his head on Trey's leg as soon as the boy was seated. Each time, after consuming the offering, Star would watch Trey for a few moments from his statue like pose, then toss his head and return to the aspen grove. That was Trey's signal to leave.

Saturday morning, Trey stuffed his warbag with flakes of grass hay and was just strapping it behind the cantle of his saddle as, true to her word, Skye rode up the long drive to his house. Trey filled a collapsible canvas bucket with grain and handed it up to Skye to strap to her saddle. With saddlebags full of food and snacks and a couple of bottles of water, they were ready for the day's adventure.

Skye followed Trey to the overhang shelter with both hands packing the grain bucket. Trey stood the war bag in the corner and rolled a sizable stone in front of it, sat the bucket beside it and sat another stone on top of the large duffle. Then reaching to the shelf he gathered the last flake of the previous load of hay, put the last couple of handsful of grain on top and the remainder of the powdered Bute around the grain. Turning to Skye, he said, "Follow me, but stay behind me. I'm going to put the hay a little closer to the stone to see if he's willing to come closer." The duo then walked the short distance to the upper part of the ravine where the slight bend in the sandy bottom turned toward the aspen grove by the spring. Each time Trey placed the feed on the ground, it was just a little closer to the boulder where he sat and observed. Today's placement was a good ten yards closer than the first, and within about ten yards of the boulder.

"Oh look, he's watching us. Look how he's standing, so proud with his head held high. He's like some chieftain that watches to see if we're worth his bother. He's so beautiful," Skye observed.

After dropping the hay and grain, they retreated to the boulder. Again, Tobey awaited his master and wiggled his stub of a tail as the two climbed to seat themselves on their observation boulder. Tobey assumed his place by his master's leg and Skye seated herself on the other side of Tobey, scratching behind his ears as she was seated. From the distant Aspen grove, Star did not miss a move of the two friends. Once they were seated and quiet, he casually walked toward the feed, dropping his head to sniff the ground while keeping his eyes on his observers. Twice he stopped and lifted his head to assure himself the observers had not changed, then stepped forward closer to his treat. The last couple of steps were very tentative, but without undue hesitation, as the food was more enticing than the observers were threatening.

After his meal was over, he again watched Trey, then turned his head slightly to look Skye over, and stood still for several minutes as if waiting for them to do something. Then he tossed his head, spun around on his right hind leg and trotted off to the grove with his mane flying and his tail held high.

"It's like he's showing off! What a strut! Look at his mane and tail. Boy would I like to get my hands on that. I'd braid them both and comb them out then he could really strut!" bragged Skye as she grinned at Trey, her excitement contagious.

His grin split his face and a low chuckle emitted from deep in his chest. "Now you're beginning to see why I've been so excited. I think we'll stay here, maybe eat our lunch right here, and just watch him. Let him get more comfortable with us being here. The more natural that becomes, I think he'll allow his curiosity to check us out and get closer. At least, that's what

I'm hoping he'll do," he related. He was glad to see Skye's excitement. He had often thought that anything someone likes, is much more special when it is shared. Her enthusiasm seemed to validate his feelings for Star. He knew the stallion was exceptional, but to have that same evaluation from someone he trusted and that knew as much or more about horses than he did, was like a stamp of approval on his judgment of the red horse.

Their lunch was venison summer sausage with crackers, string cheese and bottled water. Shared on a big rock in a narrow ravine with an aspen grove and a mountain that rose above them, the meal was far better than a gourmet serving in a fancy restaurant. The food was good, the company exceptional and the location unequaled. While they enjoyed their lunch, they continued to observe the stallion. He had strolled to the spring, took a long drink, turned to look at them, and returned to the grove. As they began to pack up the remains of their lunch, Trey whispered, "Here he comes, don't look at him."

With a nonchalant stroll, the stallion walked down the far side of the ravine, ears forward, but with a watchful eye on the two visitors. He looked at the side of the ravine, down at the gravelly bottom, occasionally dropping his head to sniff something or to take a bite of a stray clump of last season's grass. There was nothing on that side of the ravine that had received enough moisture to start an early spring green-up but he surveyed the hillside anyway. When he was even with his visitors, he turned to face them, stopped and looked directly at them with the muscles twitching in his shoulders as if anticipating the need for a quick escape. Neither Trey nor Skye looked directly at him but dropped their heads as if looking at something on the rock, and observed him with sidelong glances. The horse took a step toward them, lifted his head, and turned back toward the grove and casually returned to his retreat.

"Wow, that's the first time he has come on his own, not being bribed with food or anything. Every step is progress," whispered Trey.

"I thought for a moment there that he was going to come charging us, but he didn't," replied Skye softly.

"I think that's enough for today. Let's head on home and come back tomorrow."

Star Dancer

Chapter 11: Tutor

THE CROWD IN THE GRANDSTANDS at the edge of the indoor arena attentively watched the lone rider near the pipe fence in front of them. Attired in a long sleeved white shirt with a black string tie, a silver belly Stetson and a broad smile, Pastor Adams sat astride a Wade saddle on top of his dapple grey quarter horse gelding. The broad horn of the saddle served as the resting place for his black leather bible, now open to his text for his Sunday morning sermon from the last chapter of Matthew. His resonant baritone voice was amplified with a cordless microphone clipped to his shirt pocket and while he spoke, alternating leg pressure prompted his horse to side pass from one side of the crowd to the other and back again. Most listened closely to what the pastor was saying, but others were mesmerized by the fluid movements of his mount. Without touching the rein that lay on the neck of his gelding, the horse stopped and stood completely still at the middle point of the crowd and the pastor said, "As we close the message today, my friends, let's not forget the command of our Lord and Savior that we are to ". . . preach the gospel to every creature . . . ", in our own way, at our unique opportunities, we must share the love of Christ. Now, let us be dismissed in prayer." At an unseen que, the dapple grey bent his right front leg under his stomach, shifted his weight to his hind legs, stretched his left front leg to the front and dropped his head to the ground in what appeared to be a prayerful pose. The pastor placed one hand in front of the saddle on his horse's withers, and dismissed the crowd with a short prayer. At the word, "Amen" the grey lifted his head and stood upright, then the pastor kneed him to go to the entrance gate to greet the worshippers as they left.

Skye and her mom waited until the rest of the crowd left then approached the pastor. "Pastor, I've got a problem that you might be able to help me with. Do you have a couple of minutes to talk?"

"Of course, Skye, how can I help you?" replied the pastor.

"Well, I remember one time in one of your sermons, you said you had struggled to overcome Dyslexia, is that right?" she asked.

"Yes, Dyslexia is a condition that many people have and each one is unique. It brings challenges that are different for each person," he stated, then continued. "Do you think you have it?"

"No, but a friend of mine might, and he needs some help." Skye proceeded to tell the pastor about Trey and what his general education teacher had said and his mother's response. Skye also told him about Trey and the red stallion and what he had already accomplished. After more discussion, arrangements were made for the pastor and Skye to try to meet up with Trey and see if there might be a possibility of working together to find a solution to the challenge of the possibility of Dyslexia.

It was about two o'clock when the pastor and Skye pulled up in his jeep to the entrance of the ravine that sheltered Star Dancer. They noticed Trey's paint tethered to the juniper then stepped out to climb the boulders guarding the entrance. Leading the way, Skye walked the bottom of the ravine toward the shelter overhang, then past it to the stone perch used by Trey. The two walked quietly and slowly as they approached

64

the overlook but Trey was not there. Skye whispered, "Let's go up there and wait, we can see the rest of the ravine from there and I'm sure we'll see Trey and whatever he's up to now." She scratched her way to the stone followed by the pastor.

As they seated themselves, they looked toward the Aspen grove and spotted the stallion and Trey facing each other and both standing statue like. There was a scant two yards separating them and neither moved. The red horse had his ears forward and still, his eyes on Trey and not a muscle twitched. It was apparent the boy had carefully and deliberately approached the stallion empty handed and sought to simply show and receive trust. As if the stillness was contagious, both the pastor and Skye were completely still, hardly a breath could be heard. Although it was just a few moments, it seemed much longer. As they watched, Trey slowly turned around and with his back to the stallion, he dropped his head, removed his hat, wiped his brow and replaced his hat. He was showing trust but also disinterest, just to see how the stallion would react. Several more minutes passed, then Trey slowly began to walk away. The stallion never moved except to turn his head and watch the boy leave his space. When Trey was about five yards away, the stallion took a couple of tentative steps, as if to follow, then stopped. It was then the stallion noticed the two observers on the stone and he tossed his head and turned back to his aspen grove.

"Well, hello. I didn't expect to see you here. I thought you were going to church with your mom," commented Trey.

"I did. And I brought somebody to see you," said Skye, "Trey, this is Pastor Randy Adams, he's the pastor at the Cowboy Church in town. Pastor, this is Trey StandingElk, my friend."

"Good to meet you Trey. Say, that's an impressive sorrel you're working with. I like your approach. We don't see that gentle manner very often."

"Are you familiar with training horses?" asked Trey with a surprised look on his face. "I thought you pastors just spent your time at church and in the bible."

Skye and the pastor looked at one another and Skye turned to Trey, "You should see what he does with his dapple grey gelding. It's like the two of them are joined at the hip. Pastor here is an old rodeo hand and he practically grew up on the back of a horse."

As the pastor dropped his head and chuckled, Trey looked at him and thought, He sure doesn't look like what I thought a pastor should look like. Maybe he does have a little cowboy in him.

"Trey, I hope you don't mind, but after we talked the other night about what your mom and Mr. Whitson discussed, I got to thinking about it and I remembered something. Pastor Adams said in a sermon once that he had faced the challenge of Dyslexia and knew what it was to overcome something that can be totally overwhelming. I asked him if he would be willing to talk to you to help you understand it and maybe give you some pointers on how to meet the challenge head on. Especially after you said you thought about quitting school, I just had to do something. Will you at least talk about it? Please."

Pastor Randy had watched Trey and Skye as she spoke and he was surprised to hear her mention that Trey had thought about quitting school. That simple statement took the pastor back in time to his teen years and when he had exactly the same thought. The remembrance of that time strengthened his resolve to try his best to help Trey. Perhaps the common ground of working with horses would be the platform for their problem solving.

Trey looked up at the Pastor and said, "Well, Pastor, I know I need some help, but I'm not sure my problem is Dyslexia. I haven't been tested or evaluated or anything like that, but I know I have problems with my reading and especially when I'm around crowds." He dropped his head and stubbed the toe of his boot in the sandy ravine bottom, "But, my family doesn't have the money to pay a tutor, and my Dad would probably be upset just to think I even need one. He thinks I should stand on my own two feet without help from anyone."

"Well, Trey, I think there are times in our lives that everybody could use a little help. Sometimes the load we have to carry is just too much for one person. But I tell you what, why don't we just take it one day at a time and see where it leads us. If it helps, great, if not, maybe I can help you with Star Dancer if you want."

The idea of having an experienced trainer help with the red horse was appealing yet disquieting as well. Trey wanted to do the work with Star himself, but he knew he was not experienced enough to know all the nuances of training and it might help to have someone with him that had that knowledge and experience. He was also willing to admit that he needed some help if he was going to get through high school without making a career out of it. He turned to the Pastor and said, "O.K., that sounds good. We'll have to work out some sort of schedule I guess, but we can give it a try."

Star Dancer

Chapter 12: Introductions

THE FINAL THREE WEEKS of the school year passed quickly for Trey, not because he changed his opinion of school but because he did everything he could to finish school and get to spend time with Star Dancer. Two weeks before school was out, Trey's dad, Stoney, came home from the oil field on his days off with his rotating shift. When his wife told him about the school conference and the recommendation of the general education teacher, Mr. Whitson, his dad reacted just as expected, and voiced his opinion about the school and the teaching staff. "My son is not disabled! He's smart as a whip and can do anything he sets his mind to and do a good job of it. We're not goin' ta waste our money on no tutor or any other program they come up with. You remember what happened the last time one of them teachers had a bright idea about our son! It cost us a chunka money and didn't do him any good. He'll just have to work harder or study harder and if that don't git it done, then he can just forget school and come with me to the oil field."

Knowing it was useless to discuss it any further, Trey's mom dropped the subject and spent the rest of the week keeping peace in the family. His dad was a hard worker and a good provider but was from the "old school" of the reservation lifestyle that meant men were men and brought home the paycheck, while women took care of the family and the household. Trey didn't know exactly what his dad did in the oil field other than work on the drilling rigs. He knew his dad worked for one of the larger companies and was well respected by the crew he worked with but his dad often expressed his concern about the instability of the job. This time home he told his family that another rig had been pulled and taken to Texas and the entire crew had been laid off. So the idea of working in the oil field was not something that Trey ever seriously considered. Surely there was something that would be better for him, maybe working on a ranch or working with horses somewhere.

Trey had spent most evenings with Star and the weekends included Skye, at least on Saturdays. Most Sundays Skye attended the Cowboy Church in Lander where Pastor Adams conducted services in the indoor arena. The pastor had a busy schedule this time of year and had met with Trey just one Saturday. That time had been spent getting acquainted and talking about the main difficulty Trey experienced with his reading. He had also given Trey a couple of tips about the training of Star. But today, Skye had accompanied Trey to the ravine and the pastor said he would join them after lunchtime.

The time spent with Star had shown slow progress. Trey would bring the hay and grain and each time was able to approach closer to Star. Just the past weekend he had been able to touch the stallion without the horse spooking and running away. With each time together, the touches became longer and easier and finally just this morning he had rubbed the stallion's forehead and the horse responded by pushing back against the long strokes and lifting his head in enjoyment. Trey stepped slightly to the side and continued to stroke Star by running his hand down his neck to his shoulder and back again, all the while talking softly to the horse. He continued with the touching by rubbing Star behind the ears, which he responded to with a slight pushback and angling his head for more contact. Trey was grinning with a face splitting expression as he looked to Skye to see her response and was rewarded with a big smile and a wave. She had slowly approached the two as they enjoyed their mutual love fest and stopped about five yards in front of Star. With ears forward, Star watched as Skye approached but showed no sign of alarm as Trey continued his massage.

Tobey had been beside Trey as he first approached Star and now lay closer to the Aspen in the shade of the now sprouting white barked trees. Without concern, he watched the petting party. It had been obvious to Trey that Tobey had made greater progress befriending Star than he had as was evidenced by the friendly greetings given to the dog by the stallion. Whenever Trey arrived at the ravine, he would announce their arrival with a long whistle to Star which prompted the horse to trot to the entrance to survey his visitors. Tobey would usually outdistance Trey by diving under the makeshift fence and dashing to meet Star then running circles around him as he approached. Whether it was Star's loneliness or just his social nature, the friendship developed quickly.

Star showed his independence and signaled an end to the scratch fest by tossing his head and turning away from Trey to casually walk to the spring for a long drink. The grass around the spring was sprouting and showing green with a few scattered spring flowers peeking their buds and a few blossoms through the soft dirt. There were a few patches of bitter dogbane with pink buds trying to open scattered among clusters of Indian lettuce. The early colors of spring were showing throughout the aspen framed glen. The hillsides of the ravine had prickly pear cactus with large buds of yellow blossoms and the few bunches of hedgehog had buds with bright pink stretching the confines to show their colors. With Star stepping away, Trey chose to use the time as a lunch break and walked with Skye back to the overhang.

They were finishing their lunch when they heard the approach of the pastor's jeep. Skye turned to Trey, "See, I told you he would come. When he says he'll do something, he means it. You can always count on him, Trey." Her remarks were a result of a previous conversation with Trey when he said he didn't think the pastor really meant it when he said he would help Trey.

He stood and looked down at Skye as she rolled to her knees and started to rise, "O.K., you win," he groaned and moved toward the trail to meet the pastor. The man descending the trail toward the overhang did not resemble the usual picture of a pastor of a church. There was no white collar, no black suit, no shiny shoes and no pasty white complexion. It was a man in a grey felt hat with a snakeskin hatband, a plaid western shirt overlaid with a down filled vest that topped faded jeans held up with a silver buckled carved leather belt. Scuffed boots skidded down the steep rock strewn trail as pastor Adams dug in his heels to slow his descent. A broad smile on the leathery face showed below the friendly eyes shaded by the broad hat brim. When he made it to the bottom of the trail, two long strides brought him before Trey and his extended hand was grasped by Trey.

"Howdy guys. Looks like I missed lunch! " He dropped the strap that held a side pack on his left shoulder, "So, Trey, are ya makin' a lotta progress with your big sorrel?"

"Some. It's takin' time. We had a pretty good session of handlin' him today. I got to touch him all over his front quarters, neck, behind his ears, and all. Haven't tried much else," replied Trey.

"Hey, any progress is good progress. I'm kinda surprised he's let ya handle him that much. It usually takes a purty long time, especially for mustangs," stated the pastor. "What's next? Have you tried to put a halter on him?"

"Not yet. I've got one and I've carried it with me a couple of times, so he's seen it and smelled it, but I left it kinda tucked in my belt. I want him to get used to it first."

"Well, you're goin' 'bout it right. I found it's better to take it easy, than to rush it and have to make up for mistakes. Sometimes it's purty hard to get that trust back. So, how 'bout we take a seat on your favorite rock over yonder and we can watch him and I can show you something I want you to try."

The trio and Tobey made their way up the ravine and scratched their way to the promontory boulder for the first study session. Skye and Tobey moved to the furthermost edge of the stone giving the student and tutor room and a semblance of privacy.

"Trey, I need you to understand a couple of things as we get started. First, I'm not a professional, but I will do everything I can to help you. Second, everyone that has Dyslexia, and we're not sure that you do, is different. And because each one is different, what works for one might not work for another. But what we will do is I'm going to show you what helped me and if it works for you, great. If not, then together we'll try to find what will work. O.K.?"

Trey didn't know what he expected, but he liked the pastor's honesty and straight forward way of telling him what it was going to be, yet he still had some questions. "How long do you think it will take?"

"If you mean, how long will it take before you don't have the problem anymore, I can't answer that. I know that with most of us, Dyslexia is a life-long challenge. As we learn methods or tools to help us, it becomes a little easier to handle. And as we go through life, we each learn more things that help us overcome those challenges. Now, that's not just with Dyslexia, that's with everything in life. Every day we have challenges, some bigger than others, and we have to learn to face them and do our best to overcome them. But enough of that, I'm not supposed to be preaching. Here, let me show you something." He reached into his side-pack and pulled out a paperback Bible. He laid the book between them and began to turn the pages to a previously chosen selection.

"Here's what I want you to do. I'm going to show you this one verse, and I want you to take however much time you need, ask questions if you want, and just work out what it says. This Bible is in the New Living Translation, which means it is easier than what most think." He then pointed to the page and let his finger rest at John 3:16. "Just look at it from this number 16 and to the number 17. Take your time and if you hit a bump in the road, let me help you get over it. O.K.?"

Trey lifted the Bible to his lap and with his forefinger began to examine the verse. He silently mouthed the words and occasionally shook his head, started over and continued. Within a few moments, he said, "O.K., let me try it." Without waiting for an answer, he started, "For God doved the word so much that he gave his one and lonely Son, " he paused and looking up at the pastor, he said, "That's not right, is it?"

"Well, it's not perfect, but it's not bad. That helps me to understand what your brain is telling you. You see, Trey, those of us with Dyslexia have brains that process things a bit differently than others. It has nothing to do with intelligence, but just that our brains work differently. So we have to teach our brains to do things different and that takes time and work. So, let me show you what is different here." He then took the Bible and held it between them and began, "What I found that helps me is to listen to myself as I read that sentence, and ask myself if it makes sense or if I understand it. Now, what you said was 'For God doved' and as we think about it, does that make sense?"

Trey's forehead furrowed with the question and he mouthed the short phrase to himself, and turning to the pastor, "No, it doesn't."

"Good. Now let me show you. The word is loved, but your brain turned it around and put the d first making it doved. So as we carefully listen to ourselves, we can pick up on those things. You also said, 'lonely Son'. Now look at this word," he said as he pointed again to the page. "See, it is *only*, and again your brain mixed up the letters, but if we listen to the phrase, it says, '. . .his one and only Son'. Does that help?"

A slight smile smoothed his brow and brought light to his eyes as Trey responded, "Yeah. It does."

"It's not going to be easy. Especially at first. You'll have to really work at it but it will be worth it. I want you to take this with you and every chance you get, you work on just this one verse. If you have any problems, don't hesitate to contact me. Then the next time we'll work on it together and maybe do a little more. Just take your time and think it out," encouraged pastor Adams. "Now, show me what you can do with your big sorrel."

Star Dancer

Chapter 13: Challenges

TREY HAD PACKED a bag of apple treats in his warbag and put a hand full in his vest pocket. Star had quickly become accustomed to the treats whenever Trey approached and now lifted his head to see if Trey's hand was outstretched with a treat in his open palm. Trey had tucked the halter in his belt at his back and slowly approached the stallion. Star did not hesitate in his approach to the bearer of treats and quickly lipped the treat to his mouth. Trey rubbed the forehead of the red horse and then scratched behind his ears and stroked his cheeks and neck all to the delight of Star. He slowly reached behind his back and brought the leather halter toward Star's nose to give the horse an opportunity to sniff and investigate. Deciding this was not a treat, Star ducked his head to give Trey better access to his ears. As Trey brought the halter to the nose of the horse, Star lifted his head but did not fight his trainer. Trey reached under Star's throat to flip the top strap of the halter over his head, then quickly buckled the strap at the side. Trey continued to stroke and scratch the horse's head around and under the halter.

Pastor Adams and Skye stood to the side and about seven or eight yards away when the pastor said, "Skye, why don't you take the brush or the curry comb over and introduce Star to a little grooming." While Trey loosely held the stallion, Skye slowly approached with the curry comb in her back pocket. She started stroking Star's neck and then to his shoulders and withers, first with open palm and then using her fingers to scratch a bit. Because of the season, horses were losing their winter coat and the rubbing and scratching felt good to the dry skin. Skye scratched with her left hand then slowly introduced the curry comb. Star turned his head to see what she was doing, but the twitching of his shoulder and slight dip of his back told Skye that this would be a good way to spoil the once wild stallion.

With a soft voice, "Trey, with a light touch to the halter, see if Star will step out with you a little ways, not too far, just a couple of steps," advised the pastor.

With the slightest pressure as he turned, Trey pulled on the halter and after a slight hesitation, Star stepped out behind him. Only two steps at first, but Trey knew this was a great start. He turned and scratched Star's forehead, then reached into his vest pocket and produced a single treat, much to the pleasure of the stallion.

"Now, step to his side, and apply enough pressure to see if he'll bend his neck back to his side. First one side and then the other," directed the pastor.

With slow confident movements, Trey took a step toward Star's side, then touching him on the back and giving a little pressure with his left hand on the halter, he pulled his head back toward his side. Star yielded with little hesitation. Trey released the pressure, Star faced forward, and Trey repeated the action. First on one side, then the other, Star showed a willingness to respond to the touch and pressure of Trey. After this simple exercise, Trey looked to the pastor and was rewarded with a smile and a thumbs up signal. After about an hour of continued grooming, stroking, and flexing, the two attendants decided to call it a day. Saying their goodbyes to Star, they stepped off toward the overhang as they followed the pastor, excitedly talking about the great progress of the day. As Trey bent to put his leftover treats into the warbag, he was surprised with a push from behind that tumbled him over almost on his face. From his prone position on his back, Trey looked up to see Star shaking his head as if he was laughing at the clumsy human. He was joined in laughter by the pastor and Skye and finally by a humbled Trey.

The pastor left in his jeep while Skye and Trey rode their horses on the now familiar road to return home. It was a warm and sunny day and a few clouds slowly danced across the broad blue sky. The horses were walking with a lazy gait and occasionally dragging their hooves through the loose gravel of the roadway. The random clatter of stone and hoof stirred little dust clouds around the horses' hooves and gave a rhythmic accompaniment to the quiet thoughts of the riders. Skye looked to Trey and startled him with, "Hey! You look like you're about to fall asleep. Wake up sleepyhead, before you fall out of your saddle. Course that might knock some sense into that thick head of yours, but I'm not interested in trying to haul you all the way home. You seem to be deep in thought. Whatcha thinkin' 'bout?"

The machine gun delivery of her brief speech got his attention and he looked at her with his forehead wrinkled like the trunk of a cottonwood. "Uh, I guess I was just thinkin' 'bout Star and what I need to do with him."

"So, now that school's out, how often ya gonna come up here?"

"I'd like to come up every day, but that kinda depends on Mom's schedule and Dad's days off. The more time I spend with him, the quicker the trainin' will go. As long as I don't mess it up."

"Mess it up? You ain't gonna mess it up. You already have a bond with that horse. I've never seen one act so gentle and easy-goin' so early in the trainin'" Skye reflected.

"Today was a great day, wasn't it?"

"Yeah, it was. He's gonna be a great horse. But, don't be forgettin' your studyin' like the pastor said. You need to bring your stuff with you when you come up here, take a break, study a bit, then back at it. You know what I mean?"

Trey stretched back and put his hand on Pepper's rump, then turned to Skye and asked, "Are you gonna be able to come up with me?"

"Sometimes, but not as often as you plan on coming. I'm still working on my dance outfit for the pow-wow, and I've got to do some practicing too, so, I'll come up some. Just let me know when you're coming up and I'll see if I can."

As they approached the junction of the dirt roads nearing Trey's home, Skye turned Praline up her road and with an over the shoulder smile and wave, she spurred her horse to a lope to hurry home. Trey leaned on Pepper's neck in front of his saddle horn and spoke to his horse, "So, buddy. You ready for some oats and a good brushing? I bet you are. You're probably tired of this daily jaunt up the mountain." With a toss of his head, Pepper hastened his step toward home.

Chapter 14: Practice

THE FIRST DAY of summer break saw Trey mounted on Pepper with Tobey by their side en route to the ravine corral of Star Dancer. The trek usually took just shy of two hours, enough time for Trey to collect his thoughts and make a rough plan for the day's training. Yesterday was the best day so far and resulted in successfully haltering the stallion and increased his comfort level with both Trey and Skye grooming and handling him. As he remembered the day, a sly smile crept over his face and a chuckle bubbled from his chest. He was not overly expressive, but private thoughts about Star and Skye always brought a special joy. He thought about what he should try with the training today, knowing the response of the horse did more to dictate the action than any plans he made in advance. Picturing his stallion, he settled on working with the halter, maybe trying to lead him a little, and handling him more. Perhaps he would try to pick up his feet in preparation of a visit from the farrier.

As he approached the ravine, he had a thought about trying something different. He stepped down from Pepper and led him to the makeshift fence. With considerable effort, he loosed the ropes from around the boulder, dropped the fence at one end and led Pepper through to the inside and ground tied him. Climbing to the top of the boulder, he secured the rope and drew it tight. He noted that he would soon have to replace the branches and limbs that covered most of the fence. He led Pepper to the overhang and tethered him to the larger stones at the corner. Securing two flakes of hay and the handful of grain, he dropped one flake for Pepper then he whistled to tell Star of his arrival. The answering whinney from the stallion heralded his trotting approach to meet Trey. Stretching out to reach for the flake of hay, the stallion lifted his head in surprise as he noticed the presence of Pepper. A curious toss of his head and a throaty rumble of question from Star was answered with a nicker from Pepper. The horses eyed each other until Trey distracted the red horse by reaching out to stroke his face and speaking to him, "Easy boy. I just wanted to introduce you to a friend. You need a little company and he's going to help me teach you a thing or two."

Trey continued to stroke the neck and ears of his stallion, all the while speaking in a low soft voice to reassure him of his presence. A few minutes later as Star continued to eat, Trey turned away and returned to the overhang to get a lead rope and a curry comb. He reassured Pepper with a stroke and a "Good boy," and walked back to the stallion. With Star's nose still buried in the hay and grain, Trey reached down and clipped the lead rope to the ring in the bottom of halter. He stood with slack in the rope and again stroked the stallion's neck and back to his withers, reassuring him with a continual monologue. Tobey was belly down a few feet to the opposite side and carefully watched his master and his much larger friend. Trey lay the lead rope over the neck of the horse and waited for him to finish his meal. While Star was preoccupied with eating, Trey ran his hand down Star's neck and without breaking contact, ran his hand down the length of his front leg and back up and then repeated his motion. At first, the horse lifted his leg away slightly as if in annoyance, but then stood firm as the boy continued his stroking.

Star, finished eating, was now feeling a little anxious and curious about the other visitor and lifting his head with ears forward, he sounded another low grumble in question. Pepper's head immediately came up and looked at the challenger. Trey grabbed the lead rope with one hand by the halter and the other taking the slack in the rope. Then using the horse's curiosity to his advantage, he stepped out and gave a slight tug to the halter which prompted Star to follow. He led the stallion past Pepper and as Pepper turned to face the challenge, Trey brought the two of them closer together and allowed them to talk and sniff to get acquainted. Trey reminded them of his presence and spoke a little louder to establish his control. Then with a firm pull on the halter, he led Star away to the upper part of the ravine. Almost without realizing it, the stallion had allowed himself to be led and totally controlled by the young man. Although it was more yielding to curiosity than surrendering to the rope, the learning to respond to the lead rope was a big step. The bond between the two grew with every small victory and every yielded deed of mutual respect.

For the remainder of the morning, Trey continued to handle the stallion. He used the curry comb to smooth his still shedding coat and with the lead rope he repeated the exercises of the previous day. He would flex Star's neck to one side, back to the front, flex again then the same with the other side. He then would lead Star in a tight circle, face him the opposite direction and repeat the exercise. After each practice the horse was rewarded with additional grooming and stroking. As Trey combed the stallion's coat, he walked around him passing behind him by keeping a hand on his rump and talking so as to not surprise or spook the horse. As Star stood and enjoyed the attention, Trey stretched an arm over the stallion's back and leaned a little weight on him, then off, and on again, each time giving a little more weight to the lean. Star lifted his head and looked down the ravine with his ears forward, giving warning that something or someone was approaching. Trey heard the familiar sound of the approaching vehicle and recognized it as the pastor's jeep. Leaving the side of his horse, he walked to the entrance to greet his unexpected visitor.

As the pastor made his usual sliding entrance down the trail, Trey greeted him with, "I sure didn't expect to see you today!"

"Well, I didn't plan on bein' here, but I've got something to talk to you about. Did I make it in time for lunch?" inquired the cowboy preacher.

"Just in time. I've got a little bit of sausage and some crackers we can wash down with some bottled water, if that suits ya."

"Sounds good to me. Let's go to the sunny picnic rock and I'll tell ya' 'bout my surprise."

Trey grabbed his shoulder bag and followed the pastor to the observation rock. After both were seated and Trey brought out the venison summer sausage and crackers, they built their snacks for lunch. The pastor asked to bless the food with a short prayer and Trey quietly listened.

"So, Skye tells me you're not sure about a direction for your training. Is that right?"

"Yeah, but I've thought about several different things. Actually, I was kinda waitin' for Star to tell me which way to go," he said with a mischievous smile spreading.

The pastor dusted some cracker crumbs from his lap and said, "There's more truth to that than most people want to admit, but after watching you working with him yesterday, I had an idea you might like. I found out about a reining competition goin' on up in Cody next week and I thought you might like to go. You know, get a look at what some other trainers have done with their horses. There's several different classes and categories of competition. I think it'd give you a good idea about what you might like to do with Star."

Trey had listened so intently to what the pastor was saying, he didn't notice Tobey steal his cracker and sausage. "Wow. Yeah. I've never seen a competition like that, I would love ta go. Gee, that'd be great pastor. But, I'm not sure I'd have enough money to pay my way and I'd have to see what Mom would say. But, I'd sure like to see that," his excitement bubbling over.

"I've got a little time today, whatcha doin' with big red?"

"Well, I've put a little weight on him, and I thought about tryin' ta get on top of him," mused Trey.

"I see you've got your saddle horse in here, were you gonna use him somehow?" asked pastor Adams.

Putting the remnants of lunch back in his shoulder bag, Trey started to stand and looking at the pastor, "I'm not sure. I know some have used a primary horse to snub down a colt or something like that, but I'm not sure. Mostly I brought Pepper in for a little compny' for Star."

"What about this? You go up to Star, stay on his left side, stroke him pretty good and keep him settled down, then I'll come up with Pepper and we'll see if we can't work 'em together and maybe get you on board Star. Whatcha think?"

Trey looked sidelong at the pastor as he thought about and pictured the suggested action. Then he replied, "Yeah, I like it. I think it'll work." Trey dropped his shoulder bag at the overhang, then purposefully strode to the top of the ravine to start working with Star. As he approached, he reached into his vest pocket for the ever-present apple treats. He extended his hand with the offered treat and slowly approached the stallion while speaking lowly to the horse. Star anxiously lipped the treat from Trey's hand, while Trey once again clipped the lead rope to the halter ring. He reached to his rear pocket and grabbed the curry comb and began to comb the coat on the back of the stallion while Star would dip his back and stretch out his legs as he enjoyed the scratching of the comb that raked the loose winter coat free.

After a few minutes of combing the sorrel, first from one side and then the other, Trey crossed under the neck of Star to return to the left side. He returned the curry comb to his hind pocket and stretched his arm across Star's back, leaned his weight on him and reached down his opposite side to stroke his ribs and side on the right side and back again to the left. Star enjoyed the attention and dropped his head down and stood with eyes drooping in contentment. As Trey was standing on the left side, he did a little hop to lift himself slightly onto the back of Star. It didn't surprise Star, but it got his attention as he lifted his head and opened his drowsy eyes, then as he turned his head back to see what was going on, Trey hopped again and was successful to belly straddle the horse. The spring loaded rear legs of Star reacted in an instant and before Trey knew it, he was bouncing backwards off the stallion and came to a sudden stop on his back on the ground. Star hadn't moved his front legs and now casually turned his head to look at the prone figure of Trey, then turned slightly and dropped his head to sniff his would-be rider and lipped Trey's cheeks in what appeared to be a make-up kiss.

Trey was struggling to get up from his embarrassing placement on the ground as the pastor and Pepper approached having witnessed his performance.

With a little chuckle, the pastor said, "Is that some new style of training you're trying?"

"No, I thought I'd get down low and examine his undercarriage. You know, just to see if he's put together right," responded the grounded trainer.

"And is he?"

"Oh yeah. Real solid chassis and runnin' gear," observed Trey, with a sly smile.

"Well, latch on to him again, and let's try snubbin' him up a little and see if you can make the whistle. Ain't that only for 8 seconds?" stated the pastor, recalling the rodeo requirement for the bareback ride.

Trey stood, dusted himself off, and still holding the lead rope, again approached the stallion. Using the same tactic, he waited until the snubbing crew approached the opposite side. He reached under Star's neck and passed the lead rope to pastor Adams as he brought Pepper beside Star. The two horses muzzled each other with both muttering a rumble from their chest, but neither horse showed any aggression. The pastor kneed Pepper and the horses started a slow walk side-by-side and Trey walked beside Star. With a bit of a hop, and one hand on the patch of mane at Star's withers, Trey belly straddled the stallion. The horses continued their slow walk, but Star was sort of double stepping with the strange activity on both sides. Trey shifted his weight, swung his right leg over the rump of the stallion and sat astraddle of Star. The group of two horses and two riders continued the walk to the lower part of the ravine, crossed the sandy bottom and turned back to the Aspen grove. About 30 yards from the grove, the pastor casually handed the lead rope to Trey and slowly guided Pepper away from the stallion. Now Trey was alone astride the stallion and in sole control. His legs hung loosely to the side, he held the lead rope with his right arm resting across Star's withers. When they reached the Aspen grove, Trey used a little left leg pressure, Star turned parallel to the grove, then with a soft "whoa" the stallion stopped. Trey slipped easily to the ground beside his horse and stroked his neck and face while saying, "That's a good boy. You are an amazing horse, you know that?"

Star Dancer

Chapter 15: Routine

THE DAYS OF TRAINING and working with Star settled into a routine for Trey. Each day would see him rise early and pack his lunch and any supplies needed for the day, then head out aboard Pepper with the Australian Shepherd, Tobey, following alongside. Often, Tobey would give Trey a pleading look with a turn of his head and succeed in hitching a ride behind Trey. He would usually carry on a one-sided conversation with his dog as they traveled the familiar trail and jeep road to the ravine. As Trey verbalized his thoughts for the day, it was usually with the idea of planning out his action and work with his stallion. Very seldom did Tobey contradict the plans of the teen-aged trainer, but occasionally he would let his opinion be known in one syllable remarks that met with the approval of his master. In most conversations, Trey seldom got the last word and it was kind of refreshing to not be contradicted.

Today was Thursday, the last day before the scheduled trip to Cody and the horse show and competition. In the recent visits with the pastor, Trey had peppered him with questions regarding the types of competition and what to expect. The pastor was pleased with Trey's interest and both were excited to see this first competition of the year for Wyoming. Pastor

Adams had explained to Trey that many of the competitors came from other states and would travel throughout the summer to make as many shows as possible. Whenever a horse finished in the top ten, they received points and tried to accumulate enough points to compete in the State Championship that would be held later in Douglas, often just before the state fair and sometimes as part of the fair.

The work schedules of both his parents did not allow for much travel for entertainment or pleasure and as a result, Trey had never traveled as far as Cody. Most of his adventures were confined to his forays into the mountains on the reservation and usually in the company of Skye. As Trey thought of Skye, he remembered she said she would try to come up after lunch and maybe help him with Star. It wasn't that he needed or expected help with his training, but he always enjoyed time with Skye. She was his best friend, and as he sometimes thought, his only friend. *Hmm . . . does that make her my girlfriend? She is my friend and she's a girl and I really like her. But is she more of a sister than a girlfriend?* The sudden stop of Pepper brought Trey out of his reverie and he now realized that he had arrived at the ravine.

The routine was simple. Open the gate, lead Pepper in, close the gate, or rather the makeshift fence, and begin the day's training. Today was a little different and Trey unsaddled Pepper and took off the bridle and released him. Pepper stood waiting for his bit of hay as his reward for the trip. Trey had packed another warbag full of hay, almost a whole bale, and now divided up the flakes between Pepper and Star. The stallion had joined them at the overhang in response to the usual whistle and Trey dropped the flakes near one another so the two horses were closer than normal. Each dropped his head, but not without inspecting each other, then began to focus on the food instead.

The past several days, Trey had been able to hop aboard Star and ride around the ravine bareback. Before riding, he would replace the leather halter with a bosal and hanger. The braided rawhide nosepiece of the bosal is fitted to the horse in a manner that allows it to rest quietly until the rider uses the reins to give a signal. It acts upon the horse's nose and jaw. Held on the head with a simple leather hanger that resembles a bridle, the large knot at the base held a mecate, or a braided horsehair rope type rein that is usually long enough to be a loop rein and the excess being used as a lead rope as necessary. What pleased Trey, was Star needed little encouragement from the bosal and usually responded better to simple leg pressure. Trey had also been wearing moccasins instead of boots and would hook his toes behind the elbows of Star to give cues as to movement. Horse and rider had an exceptional connection and seemed to communicate with one another by simple pressures and movements.

After making several circuits of the ravine and trotting his way back to the aspen grove, Trey dropped off the back of Star, replaced the bosal with the halter and rubbed down his stallion using a brush instead of the curry comb. Star's coat had become slick and shiny and he enjoyed the softer touch of the brush and allowed Trey to comb through his mane and tail with a handled comb. Pepper and Tobey had wandered up to join the two and stood amiably by to watch. Pepper showed his jealousy by pushing his head against Trey's back and nibbling at his elbow with his lips. "O.K., O.K, I'll brush you. I know you deserve it just as much. After all, you carried both me and Tobey up here. Hang on a minute and it'll be your turn." He then turned and began grooming his faithful gelding. After tending to the horses, Trey retreated to the overhang, picked up his shoulder bag and walked back to his observation stone and makeshift dinner table. He pulled out the usual sausage and crackers and began to build his lunch. Then reaching back into his bag, he brought out the Bible to start his routine of study. With a cracker sandwich in one hand, he flipped pages in the Bible until he came to the assigned verse. He started reading and re-reading the verse. As the pastor had instructed, he would read the verse, think about what he was reading, or what he perceived, and think about it to be certain it made sense. If not, he would review it again, and again analyze the words he read. After the continued study, Trey realized he had actually memorized the verse and knew that wasn't helping him "train his mind" as the pastor instructed. So, he reread the assigned verse and continued on to the next one. *"God sent his Son into the world not to judge the world, but to save the world through him."* But as was the usual case, the verse was a bit mixed up and Trey began his study and re-read the verse, sounding it out in his mind, re-reading, analyzing for meaning, and reading again.

His study was interrupted by the sound of an approaching vehicle. It was different from the pastor's jeep and he knew it must be the farrier he talked to about working on Star. He dropped down from the boulder and walked to the entrance of the ravine just in time to see Skye sliding down the trail and followed closely by the farrier. When she stopped her descent, she smiled up at Trey, "Hey guy. Look who I brought! He was shoeing our horses and said he was him up!"

The farrier sat down his wooden tool box and extended his hand. "Howdy, I'm Jeremy Thacker. We talked on the phone but I think this is the first time we've met, you are Trey aren't you?"

"Yup, that's me. Thanks for coming up. I know this is a little out-of-the-way for you and I appreciate you makin' the trip."

"So, this horse is a mustang? And it's never had its feet trimmed or been shod?"

Trey looked up at him, kind of expecting him to back out of the deal of working on Star, "That's right. But I've been working with him and pickin' up his feet an' all."

"I see you've got another horse here, did you want me to work on him too? Cuz if you do, and we do him first, it might help your mustang see what's goin' on and not be too spooked."

Trey grinned at the slender man as he strapped on his leather chinks to ready himself for the work on the horses. He responded with, "Sounds good. I'll go get Pepper . . ."

The farrier interrupted him with, "No, let's go up there and work them together in the area where they're comfortable. Here, carry my tool box for me."

Trey reached for the wooden dowel handle that stretched from end to end of the long tool box and lifted it to his side, then stepped out behind the farrier. As they walked, Jeremy looked over his shoulder at Trey and asked, "How long ya been workin' with this mustang?"

"Uh, it's been a little over a couple a months, I think. 'bout that, anyway."

As they approached the horses lifted their heads to view the visitors to their sanctuary, then recognizing Trey and Skye, they relaxed their stance and Pepper took a step in their direction. Trey snapped the lead rope to Pepper's halter and led him a couple of steps to a level part of the hump of grass by the spring. Star stood his ground and observed from the distance. He watched as Jeremy lifted first one hoof between his knees and cleaned it out, then with the pincers he easily trimmed the hoof. Placing the hoof on the stand he used the rasp to round it out and shape it up. Jeremy stood up, reached behind his back and muttered, "I must be getting old, or sumpin'" Within a half an hour, Jeremy finished the trimming on Pepper with the final rear hoof dropping to the ground. Then with a stroke down his back, the farrier said, "Now, that wasn't so bad, was it big boy?"

Star had casually walked closer to satisfy his curiosity about the business end of the operation taking place with Pepper in the center. When the farrier finished with Pepper, Trey unclipped the lead rope and slowly approached the stallion. Trey stretch out a hand holding an apple treat and Star closed the distance between them with his extended head and opening lips. Anxiously taking the treat, he showed no resistance to Trey as he clipped the lead rope to the halter.

93

Jeremy watched the movement of the horse and looked at the hooves of the mustang. Assuming the best, Jeremy approached the stallion and after stroking his neck and his back, he then slid a hand down his leg to the fetlock and ergot to urge Star to lift his leg. After a little tug by the farrier, the stallion lifted his hoof and yielded to the hands of Jeremy as he placed the hoof between his knees and began his work. Surprisingly, the work on Star's hooves went without any complications, other than an occasional turn of his head and a nibble on the back pocket of the farrier with searching lips of a curious mustang. As Jeremy stood after dropping the last hoof, he said, "If anybody'd told me that the first trim on a mustang would go that easy, I'd called 'em a liar. If that don't beat all. I've had rich folk's high priced pet horses give me more trouble than that horse did. You've done some good work with him, boy." Although it was an off handed compliment, Trey was happy to hear it. From the mouth of a real cowboy, little praise is high praise, and Trey was thrilled. He knew Jeremy was not only a farrier, but an experienced horse trainer as well and praise from someone like him was not readily given.

As he undid his chinks and reached for his tool box, he turned to Skye, "Are you ridin' back with me?"

"Nah. Go ahead. I'm gonna go back with Trey, if he'll let me ride double with him. That is if Tobey doesn't mind," stated Skye.

Trey smiled at her and said, "I think it's more if Pepper doesn't mind. But since you've been there before, I don't think he'll object."

After the farrier left, Trey brought Pepper to the overhang to put on the bridle and saddle and put away the other supplies. Since he wasn't going to be back until the day after tomorrow, he didn't want anything to get scattered around or misplaced. He placed a larger flake of hay at the corner of the overhang away from the warbag and other gear, placed a few rocks around the gear and led Pepper to the fence. As Skye held Pepper, Trey dropped the rope from the boulder to let Skye and

Pepper exit, then secured the rope again and dropped down to join his friends. He mounted Pepper, moved his foot from the stirrup and offered it to Skye who did a little hop step, put her foot in the stirrup and swung a leg over Pepper's rump and settled herself behind the cantle of the saddle. Skye hooked her fingers in the side belt loops of Trey's jeans for a bit of stability as Pepper rocked his hips down the trail.

"So, are you gonna be ready on time in the morning? Ya know, six o'clock comes kinda early," asked Skye.

Trey turned to look over his shoulder at her, "Whatdaya mean?"

"Well, pastor said he'd pick us up at your house at six!"

"Us? You goin' too?" questioned Trey with and incredulous look on his face.

"Well, of course, silly. You don't think I'd let you go to a horse show without your assistant trainer, do ya'?"

Trey turned back forward to hide his smile from Skye, but he was happy to hear she was going with them on this big adventure.

Star Dancer

Chapter 16: Showtime

SKYE SNATCHED HER SHOULDER pack from the front step and scrambled into the Jeep climbing into the back seat. Seating herself behind the passenger seat, she noted the small cooler in the seat beside her. The pastor had said he was going to bring some sandwiches and assorted snacks to see them through the day and all the teens needed to bring was enough bottled water for the trip. Skye turned and opened the cooler and seated the bottles around the ice as Trey handed them back to her. Within a few moments, the trio was on their way for the big day's adventure. Skye's excitement bubbled over as she asked, "Pastor Adams, what type of competition is this we're gonna see today?"

"Well, Skye, there will be two basic competitions today. First will be the Versatility Ranch Horse competition, and then in the afternoon will be the different Reining classes," explained the pastor.

"So, just what is the Versatility Ranch class, what do they do?" inquired Trey.

The pastor began to explain in detail the different classes that would be shown and judged for the day. Beginning with the Versatility, he explained the different events that made up the entirety. "Versatility is to judge a horse on everything that he would be required to do as a working ranch horse. The first class is the standard judging when all the horses will be brought into the arena and stand to be judged for build, conformation, and temperament by the selected judges. They are ranked in placement with the top five getting points as they place. Then, and this order can vary, because larger shows will break the group up into smaller groups so that different events will be going on simultaneously, perhaps the next will be the cutting. Each horse and rider will have to go into a pen with several head of cattle, then cut one out away from the others, take it down the fence away from the herd, turn it and then take it back, all while maintaining control.

"The other events include a trail course which includes obstacles, sometimes crossing a stream and a bridge, loading into a trailer, backing into an given enclosure, and other things like that. Then there's the contained course that might include small jumps, opening and closing a gate, and general maneuvering through the course. There is also an event that includes roping a steer or calf and dragging it to the specified location similar to a branding. All of these events can earn points for the horse and awards are given for the events and the top award is for the overall point getter."

Trey had intently listened to the explanations and now asked, "And, what's the reining classes that you mentioned?"

"There's basically two classes. The standard class where each rider and horse has to negotiate a prescribed course and certain moves, like a spin, sliding stop, rollback, running a figure eight to change leads, that type of thing. The other class is usually held last and it's the free style. The free style is when the rider has more freedom and can do the moves to music and with a costume and the moves are not in a prescribed order. But, the same moves have to be incorporated into the choreography for a complete performance. Personally, I like the free style the best because it shows more of the relationship between the horse and rider. Often the contestants do much of the program without a bridle and using only leg cues."

Trey turned to look out the side window and sat quiet for several moments. The pastor could tell that the young man was picturing the competition and in what class or event he and Star would be most effective. He had developed a special rapport with Star and their communication was developing through touch and spoken word. Seldom did he use the bosal or rein or lead rope to control the horse, it was all done through leg pressure or a touch near his withers on the side of his neck or with his toes behind the elbows. He could envision the two of them in the type of competition where they could do their own style and performance.

With their immediate curiosity satisfied, the pastor changed the subject by asking Trey, "So, how's your studying going, Trey?"

"Well, I think I'm making progress. I believe I'm understanding the text better. Course, I have to re-read it several times and give it plenty of thought, but it's working for me."

Skye was listening to the conversation, but was also enjoying the scenery of the Wind River canyon on the way to Thermopolis. Much of the area was still part of the Wind River Indian Reservation and she enjoyed looking at the steep canyon walls and she was especially enamored with the opposite side of the river and the areas where extremely large boulders had fallen down to the river's edge and remained in place as if put there by some great power long ago. It was easy to imagine the time of many years past when it would not be unusual to see small villages of teepees erected at the water's edge with horses grazing in the small grassy meadows and children playing in the common areas. She thought of the dances she performed at pow-wows that told of the history of the people and special events of their history, and often wondered what it would have been like to live in those simpler times. The pastor's voice brought her back to the present as he said, ". . . and she referred to it as the Gift of Dyslexia."

"The gift? How so?" asked Trey.

"Well, those with Dyslexia often think or visualize in three dimensions. Where most think of the surface thought and the time line or progression of the sentence, she believes that Dyslexics see things in more of a visual figurative way. That's why many people that are Dyslexic are also very accomplished. For example, Thomas Edison, Alexander Graham Bell, and Albert Einstein and you'd be surprised at how many T.V. and movie stars also have the gift of dyslexia."

Hearing this, Skye piped in, "Pastor, when Trey and I went to see the petroglyphs, he looked at the figures and read it like a book and I had a hard time trying to figure that out. Is that what you mean?"

"Well, that sounds right. You see, the figures allowed Trey's brain to visualize the story better and he was able to put it into the story that was told by the ancients," explained pastor Adams. The discussion continued as the miles whispered under the wheels of the Jeep and the curious explorers. They entered Cody from the South and traveled through the town to the Northwest edge to the location of the rodeo arena that was the site of the day's events. As they found a parking space in the main lot, they exited the vehicle and Trey watched as some late arriving contestants and their variety of rigs consisting of pickups pulling goose-neck horse trailers, some with living quarters, pulled to the contestant area behind the announcer's stand. Trey knew these vehicles were expensive but he admired the combination of vehicles and thought, *Mebbe someday.*

"Let's head over to the grandstands and get a program of the day's events. They won't all take place in the arena and we'll get an idea what we want to see and where it will be," stated the pastor. Without comment, Trey and Skye fell in step with their leader and mentor, anxious for the day's events to begin. Many of the contestants were already leading their horses into the arena where the initial judging would start the day's program. With this being the first show of the season for the state of Wyoming, there were several horse owner's wanting to get a good start on the show season and make a good standing. Shortly after getting their seats, Trey and Skye started pointing out different horses and commenting on their appearance and behavior. The loudspeaker belched out the initial directions to the contestants telling them to form a line along the South fence facing the grandstand so the judges could get started.

The teens soon grew restless watching the monotonous movement of the judges as they walked around each horse, running their hands over the backs and down their legs in their examination of the animals. As the two read the program, they began to plan what activities were more interesting and where they would need to be to observe those events. Soon enough, the judging completed, the horsemen and women led the horses back to the trailers to saddle them for the other competitions. Pastor, Trey and Skye were most interested in the trail course that was to take place in the large field to the Northeast of the arena so they left their seats to seek a good observation place. As they arrived at the location indicated in the program, they noted there were no grandstands or other seating so they seated themselves on one of the boulders that had been used to separate the driveways from the neighboring field. It was evident the beginning point of the trail course was at the edge of the boulder barrier and they anxiously awaited the first contestant.

The first contestant was mounted on a tall palomino gelding, the rider a woman that handled the horse with confidence. At the first stop the rider dismounted and led the horse to load into a trailer then back out again, which was done seamlessly. Remounting, the course led her across a small wood plank bridge that clattered loudly as the horse's hooves met the planks. After crossing the bridge, she backed the horse between two large parallel poles laying on the ground, then spurred her horse forward to the next point where she had to loose her rope and drop a loop over the plastic steer head at the end of the hay bale and drag the bale at least ten feet. An attendant then removed her rope which she had to coil "on the go" to her next station which was on the other side of a small pool of muddy water. After crossing through the water she maneuvered her horse through a zig-zag barrier of trees and through a few willow bushes, and then on the run return to the starting point. The palomino performed flawlessly and the rider and horse received considerable applause. After watching four more horses maneuver the course with varying degrees of success and time, the trio of observers agreed that it was time to check out one of the other classes.

The large stock pen situated between the arena and the field with the trail course was the site of the cutting competition that was next on the agenda. Most of the observers sat on the fence to the South side of the large pen, while the action was taking place on the other three sides. As they found a spot on the top board of the fence, they watched as a pot-bellied man astraddle a chocolate brown mare that appeared too small for him, anchored his bottom to the saddle as the little horse showed an unexpected quickness. When he rode the horse into the small herd of cattle, the horse and rider agreed on a brindle steer that stood against the fence. As the horse pushed his way between the steer and the herd, the steer dropped his head and tried to dart past the horse only to be surprised at the quick reflex of the mare as she planted both feet in front of the steer to turn it back. Trying for the other side, again the steer was disappointed and stopped with the exact opposite move of the quick little brown horse. Then with a nudge of its chest, the mare pushed the steer to move along the North fence to the other end of the pen. As the steer broke into a run trying to outdistance the horse, the little brown quickened its pace and kept the steer between the fence and her shoulder. When they reached the end of the pen, the steer slowed its movements as the brown continued to push him slowly along the East fence, then turn the steer and take it all the way back to the herd, siding the fence and under complete control. Upon completion, horse and rider accepted the applause of the impressed crowd. They finished the morning watching the obstacle course and the roping competitions before returning to the Jeep for a much anticipated lunch.

"What do you think so far, Trey?" queried the pastor, between bites of his sandwich and chips. Tipping a water bottle to his lips, he watched Trey's response and awaited his review.

"It's great just to see so many well trained horses. I couldn't help but think about the many hours and months these people get to spend with their mounts in training and just taking care of them. And then the money it takes to travel to all these shows, wow."

"So, what part impressed you the most, and you too, Skye, what about you."

Skye jumped into the discussion with her usual enthusiasm, "I liked the cutting horse part. The way those horses moved and controlled the cattle was great. I can see where it would be a challenge just to stay aboard those horses."

Trey nodded his head in agreement, finished his sandwich then said, "I liked the trail course. But that's more of what I do all the time goin' up in the mountains. I'm lookin' forward to the reining. I want to see what that's all about."

"I'm kinda partial to the reining too. It's gonna start here in a little bit, so if you're done stuffin' your face, let's head back to the grandstands," the pastor said as he put the fixings of lunch back in the cooler. "This will be easier cuz we get to sit in one place and watch the whole shebang."

The reining started with last year's champion, a Gillette man mounted on a dapple grey introduced as the two entered the arena on a fast run from the West end of the arena toward the East end, upon reaching a designated point the rider sat back in the saddle and the horse dropped both hind legs under him and dug his hooves in the loose dirt while continuing to walk with his front legs. After stopping they did a rollback with the horse swiveling by bringing his front quarters around to the left and heading in the opposite direction. They took off on a run and repeated the stop at the other end of the arena, but upon stopping the rider backed his horse several feet straight back before doing another rollback then going to a point at the center of the fence in front of the grandstand. Turning away from the grandstand and from a dead stop, the rider and horse started a spin with the left rear foot anchored and spinning around several times very rapidly without moving the anchored foot. Coming to a complete stop facing the announcer, they repeated the action in the other direction. Upon completion, they stepped out to do a large figure eight that encompassed the whole of the arena, doing this at a fast lope and changing leads at the center crossing of the figure eight. (Changing leads is changing the lead foot when changing from a right circle to a left).

Trey and Skye were both mesmerized by the fluidity of the movements of the horses and the way the horse and rider were connected as one. After watching several of the contestants, Trey asked, "So, the free style uses these same exercises or movements as part of their competition?"

"Yes, but they do it in whatever order or even with additional moves that make their program more appealing. It's going to start pretty soon," replied pastor Adams.

The free style began like the reining with the introduction of last year's champion. The entry by a long-haired blonde woman wearing a long silky white and gold costume with a frilly cape floating behind her as she sat aboard a dark palomino caught the attention of the entire crowd. Accompanied by a musical score of a large orchestra, the horse seemed to prance in time to the music as they made their way to the center of the arena. Performing the spins, they broke out of the spins and at a full run did the sliding stop with a rollback and with a smooth transition went into the figure eights with the lead changes. Coming out of the circular movements, the duo ran toward the grandstand and did another sliding stop and backed across the entire arena. With a side pass move (where the horse side steps by crossing over the front legs but without changing its orientation) they turned into an around the arena pass with her cape flying and the music coming to a big crescendo as they exited the arena.

As the palomino and rider performed the program, Trey continued to slowly slide forward on the seat as if trying to get closer and see more. Skye watched his intense involvement and motioned to the pastor to watch Trey's reaction. When the horse and rider exited the arena, Trey took a deep breath and sat back without removing his gaze from the arena. The pastor smiled at Skye and she smiled back as the two conspirators basked in their success at involving Trey so completely. The euphoria of the moment was broken as the announcer broadcast the next contestant, "And from Lander, Wyoming, aboard his horse, Windjammer Dunit, Mark Blackman."

Trey and Skye looked at each other, then both turned to the pastor. With a questioning look, he returned their stare with an unspoken, *what?* Skye briefly explained the history between Trey and Mark and about the confrontation and harassment at school.

"I didn't even know he had horses. I sure didn't think he was into anything but basketball," stated Trey.

Skye touched his arm, "Wait, let's see if he's any good. Let's watch his program."

The music sounded like it came from a John Wayne movie but neither one knew the name of the song. Mark entered dressed like an old time matinee cowboy with fringed gloves and coat with a tall peaked hat. They didn't know if he was portraying Buffalo Bill or some other old time cowboy. His horse was a well built buckskin gelding with flowing black mane and tail and he performed the requested maneuvers quite well. Although in a different order than the previous champion, the two executed the program with good timing and smooth movements. The crowd was pleased but the program was not as impressive as the woman on the palomino.

With his elbows on his knees, Trey dropped his head to look between his feet. Then turning to the pastor, he said, "I think I really like the free style. Will you help me get all those moves down?"

With a broad smile, the pastor replied, "I'd be more than happy to, Trey. But, I think we'll both need Skye's help too. Don't you think?"

Trey turned to his long time friend and slapped her on her knee, "Well, that goes without sayin' don't it partner?"

Chapter 17: Cougar

THE SCREAM SPLIT the blackness of the night like a bolt of lightning that heralds a coming storm. Star's body tensed as the warning of danger swept through him. His head came up, his ears forward and eyes wide with his entire spirit alert. Frozen in place without the slightest movement and not so much as drawing breath, he scanned the surrounding hillsides. Minimal light came from the cloud hidden moon, but he carefully examined his surroundings for any sign of movement or any additional sound that would speak of the approach of the dangerous predator. Recognizing the cry and scream of a mountain lion, Star knew the life of any living being within the sound of that screeching growl was in peril. He struggled with the decision of fight or flight and trotted away from his usual sanctuary of the aspen grove.

Previous days had seen him wear a path around the perimeter of his enclosure as his anxious manner tried to while away the time between visits from his trainer. Trotting down that path, he kept an attentive eye on the hillsides for any sign of impending attack. His head held high and his eyes so wide that the surrounding whites seemed to glow in the dark, he was driven by fear and anticipation. Within a few yards of the overhang, a flash of yellow at the corner of his eye startled the stallion to an immediate action, dropping his head between his front feet and springing his hind quarters up in a buck and kicking out. He felt a stabbing pain to the side of his back near his hip as well as a solid contact with both his hind feet. The lion sprang from a large rock outcropping attempting to sink his claws into the back of the stallion and bring him down with his weight and bite, but the buck and kick were perfectly timed, catching the cat at the instant of contact and with all the force of his hind legs, launched the cougar into the air flipping end for end and coming down on his back across part of the escarpment. Star whirled to face the danger and as the carcass of the lion impacted the stone, the stallion reared up and brought both front feet down on the struggling cougar. Again he reared, screamed and plunged down in a desperate move to destroy his attacker. Baring his teeth and with ears laid back, the next rear brought down feet and teeth to strike the death blow to the would-be assailant. The viciousness of Star's attack would have terrified any onlooker into thinking the horse was the predator and the lion the victim.

Star nervously pranced back and forth, with an occasional spin on his hind legs combined with a rear and another scream. Even the presence of the dead body of the lion and the smell of the predator caused the stallion to seek to escape. Charging at the rope and branch fence at the ravine's entrance, the makeshift fence gave way with the first impact. Slightly entangled with the rope, Star spun and fought himself free. Realizing he was no longer restricted the horse arched his neck and lifted his tail high and dug in his hooves to hasten his escape, running free through the black night.

Trey was anxious to see Star again and start with the training on the unique maneuvers that impressed him during the free style competition. He easily envisioned the two of them doing those very moves and more besides in the free style exercises. Already planning on entering the first competition once the maneuvers were mastered, he allowed his daydreaming to distract him from the trail. Pepper and Tobey were so familiar with the chosen path that neither animal strayed from the intended trail and destination. The stutter step of Pepper and the deep rumbling from his chest brought Trey out of his reverie and focused his attention on the entrance to the ravine. The fence was down! But something else alarmed Pepper as he tensed every muscle and hesitated with each step. Trey spurred him forward, making their way over the downed fence and into the ravine. On the alert and searching for anything amiss, the three watched carefully for any danger. Tobey was the first to sound an alarm as he ran forward, slunk backwards with his front feet stretched in front of him as his chest touched the ground, he barked and growled with his eyes forward to the ground and something sprawled by a large rocky escarpment. Again, Pepper rumbled a warning from deep in his chest, stopped in place and looked with alarm at the target of Tobey's angry bark. Refusing to move forward and trembling with a nervous jitter, Pepper stood his ground as Trey stepped down from his mount.

Slipping his hunting knife from his belt scabbard, Trey cautiously stepped forward. Now even with Tobey, he was able to see the cause of alarm. The inert body of a large mountain lion lay in the shade of the large boulders. Stopping in place to observe the form, he reassured himself the animal was dead, then moved closer to examine the bloody body. He kicked at it for further reassurance and without any reaction from the fur pile, his shoulders dropped as he relaxed and spoke to his companions. "Don't worry guys, he's dead. Looks like Star pounded him into the ground." At the mention of the stallion's name, he turned to look around the now empty ravine. At an anxious trot, he hastened to the end of the ravine to the aspen grove, with a searching look giving him the answer to his unasked question, Trey's heart seemed to drop from his chest. Running back to the overhang, he surveyed the area and noted that Star had scrounged his way into the hay stash and even some of the grain. But most of the supplies remained and he filled his pockets with the treats from the hidden bag on the shelf, put a couple of hands full of grain in his spread open handkerchief and returned to Pepper.

"Come on guys. Let's go find Star!" With a stretch of his leg he planted his foot in the stirrup and Pepper started out before Trey's rear hit the seat. Tobey raced ahead eagerly distancing himself from the fearsome carcass. The tracks of the stallion were easily seen as his running flight dug his hooves deep for the escape. The horse hunters followed his trail carefully but without delay. Trey noted the tracks were leading to the mesa just East of the jeep trail that was used to travel to and from the ravine. Remembering the mesa as the location where he and Skye had spotted the stallion that first night as he danced on the stars, Trey was hopeful they would find him there again.

Traversing the trail to the top of the mesa, Trey stopped to look around for his mustang. He whistled as he always did when coming to the ravine, the same greeting that always brought Star for his treats. With no response, the trio continued to move along the perimeter of the mesa, searching through each grove of trees and every dip in the terrain. Whistling and calling his name, Trey anxiously looked for any movement that would tell of the presence of his stallion. Although there was no evidence of injury to his horse at the scene of the battle, Trey could not help but fear that Star was lying somewhere in hiding because of an open wound or other injury. He whistled again, waited for a response, and whistled again. Turning in his saddle to survey as much of the terrain of the mesa as he could, he stood in his stirrups and whistled as loud as he was able. Wetting his lips and puckering again, he drew a deep breath and heard what he thought was a whinney in the distance. He faced the direction he thought the sound came from and searched the scrub pinion and scattered sage brush. He whistled again, and waited. Afraid to move or even breathe, he froze in place and waited. Another whistle. Then he heard it, that familiar whinney and trotting up from a distant draw came the familiar red horse, head held high and mane and tail flying in the wind. The smile split the face of Trey as he thought, *there he is, finally!* Swinging his leg over the saddle horn and the neck of Pepper, Trey dropped to the ground and ran toward his stallion. Sliding to a stop with his head held out and lips moving, Star sniffed for his expected treat.

The halter was in place and Trey brought the lead rope from the back of his belt and clipped it to the metal ring. The petting and stroking continued as Tobey ran circles around the red horse and even Pepper rumbled a greeting as he tossed his head. "Boy, it's good to see you. You had me scared Star. Did that lion hurt you? Let me look you over," Trey spoke softly and reassuringly to his horse. Running his hand down one leg and the other, Trey felt Star's neck and withers, ran his hand along his side, down to his belly and then to the other side. As he approached the hind quarters, he first felt the blood, and then examined the wound. A large but not too deep claw mark just forward of his right hip seemed to be the only injury suffered by the big stallion. "We need to get you home and get that doctored. We can't be gettin' it infected."

Trey remounted and leading the stallion close beside him, the small group started down the mesa to the road and homeward. Trey was so relieved, he often leaned over to stroke Star and speak to him. Midday saw them arrive at home and to the corral that had been the exclusive domain of Pepper. Trey stepped down, opened the gate and turned Star into the corral. As Star examined his new quarters, Trey unsaddled Pepper and led him into the corral with his friend. With a closer examination of the wound, Trey knew a good cleaning and application of the bag balm should hasten the healing without any complications.

Star Dancer

Chapter 18: Maneuvers

ENTERING THE ARENA was like stepping into another world. There was no one around, the parking lot was empty and the holding pens were devoid of any animal life. There was a quiet about the large arena. This was the location of the many team ropings and rodeos held under the reservation authority. Located in Fort Washakie, it was just a couple of miles from Trey's home and Star's corral. The large wide open space of the level sandy soil surrounded by the pipe fence gave unrestricted area for Trey to work with Star. This was what was needed for the next phase of training that would be necessary for the fulfillment of Trey's dream to compete in the Free Style Reining competition. After seeing the horse show competition with Pastor Adams and Skye, Trey hadn't stopped thinking about what Star would be able to do in that kind of program.

It was the guidance of Pastor Adams that started Trey to visualizing his future. Before, he would think of details, problems, and obstacles when any idea was put before him. It didn't matter if it was a subject in school or a chore to do at home, the negativity that filled his mind always brought him to a stalemate of confusion and frustration. But when the pastor explained that Dyslexia was simply a different way that his brain worked and not a disability, he was easily guided into the practice of visualizing and analyzing any challenge to be overcome. When he saw the Free Style reining competition, his free thinking mind was unleashed in a way he had never before experienced. He couldn't explain it, but it was like seeing a video in his mind that included all the steps and results of an implemented plan for his training of Star. Now, he was anxious to immerse himself and his horse in this envisioned challenge.

Trey rode Pepper and led Star into the arena while Tobey ran from one end to the other sniffing and checking out every corner of the oval arena. Trey tossed the lead rope over the neck of Star and rode Pepper to the gate of the corner holding pen. Leaning down and opening the gate, he gigged Pepper into the pen, dropped from the saddle, loosened the cinch and let Pepper roam the pen. Trey then returned to the Arena and Star. With a whistle and an outstretched hand palming an apple treat, he awaited Star.

Replacing the halter with the bosal, Trey slipped the mecate rein over Star's neck and let the excess rest across his back. The bond and communication developed between the two was unseen by any observer as the slight leg pressure, or shift in weight, or soft spoken command were so subtle as to not be recognizable by others. The two companions stepped up to a canter or lope as they circled the perimeter of the arena. It was a self-introduction to their new terrain and environment. The easy gait of the horse enabled Trey to ride without hand hold. The bosal was an unnecessary accouterment but its presence reassured Trey of the control and training tool. Thinking of the need for lead changes, where the horse leads with opposing front feet depending on the direction of lean or turn, Trey now prompted Star to a diagonal move across the arena. As they approached the far end, the lean of Trey to the right or inside of the anticipated turn for a circle and a slight nudge with his right toe to the elbow of the right leg, a slight skip in pace quickly showed the change in lead to his right leg.

Continuing through the circle into what would be a figure eight, after crossing the center and starting a left circle, Trey duplicated his weight shift and toe nudge and immediately was rewarded with the accompanying lead change by Star. This practice of figure eights and lead changes continued, with occasional breaks, for the remainder of the morning. When time for a lunch break arrived, so did Skye and the pastor, however this time, they brought the food. As Trey brought Star to a stop by the entry gate, he threw a leg over Star's neck and dropped lightly to the ground and gave a rewarding hug and forehead rub to his mount.

After greetings were exchanged, the trio walked to the bleachers to do some damage to the contents of the lunch cooler.

"So, what have you been working on today?" inquired the pastor as he continued to build his sandwich with the cold cuts and home-made sourdough bread.

Trey didn't waste any time putting his lunch together and now had to manage a face full of food before he could respond. As he finished his first sampling he replied, "Well, Star has been teaching me how to do the figure eights with smooth lead changes. I thought it was going to be pretty difficult, but I graduated grade school and he has promoted me to high school already!"

"I noticed he's a pretty good teacher, but of course, it's good that you can pick things up pretty quick yourself," the pastor kidded. "What are you going to work on this afternoon?"

"I thought I'd try those sliding stops, but I'm still thinkin' 'bout how to do them. Got any suggestions?" he asked expectantly.

While the pastor and Trey discussed the strategy for training, Skye stepped down to the pipe fence where Star stood three legged and with his eyes closed, patiently awaiting his master. Skye reached between the top rails to scratch Star's face and behind his ears, then reaching into her back pocket, she brought out a long carrot and offered it to the stallion. After sniffing it thoroughly, he cautiously lipped the carrot, then with a resounding chomp he partook of the offering. Without any further hesitation, he quickly lipped and took the remainder and with just a couple of chews, happily swallowed his treat. Bringing another one from her hind pocket, Skye endeared herself to the red horse with the simple treat.

Now remounted, Trey prepared to follow the pastor's suggestion about introducing Star to the sliding stop. Starting at the roping chute end of the arena, he started Star straight down the length of the arena at a trot, gigged him up to a canter and approaching the opposite end, brought a little pressure on the bosal while shifting his weight back and down while putting his toes just behind the elbows. Star responded with a walking stop without sliding.

The pastor said, "Now do it again, but accentuate your movements and make the pressure on the bosal more sudden and firm."

Trey and Star turned and started back the length of the arena. Quickly stepping to a lope the distance was covered in seconds. As calculated, Trey initiated the stop with a quick firm tug on the mecate rein while dropping his weight back. Star responded immediately as Trey observed from his elevated position passing over the head of his stallion. The sudden stop on his back in front of his horse knocked the air from his lungs and momentarily paralyzed Trey. Then with a gasp, spitting the dust and dirt from his opened mouth, he rolled to the side and brought his knees up then looked up at a stationary Star that was observing him with what appeared to be smile. Trey knew if horses could laugh, he would hear a good one about now. From the bleachers he heard a smattering of applause amid open laughter and muffled remarks about learning to be a cowboy. He stood up, stroked his mount's neck and ears, and said, "Good one." Then walking over to the bleachers to see his admirers, Trey asked for a bottle of water to wash down the remaining dust and dirt.

"Like you said, he's a good teacher. Course, some lessons are a little harder than others," smirked Skye, as she tried to stifle a chuckle that soon erupted into an extended laugh.

"Now Trey, you will need to have a farrier put sliders on Star before you do that too much. Sliders are a longer horseshoe and a little wider, depending on the make, and smooth to make it easier when your horse sits down on his hind end and slides. The front set will be the normal ones because you don't want him sliding on all four," explained the pastor.

"O.K. I can see that. By the way, I wanted to ask you about this Free Thinking thing. You said it's where we envision the whole picture of anything instead of just the surface words or problem, is that right?"

"You're on the right track. Everybody is different, but by seeing the whole picture or more than most, it enables you to solve the problem or whatever you're faced with," replied pastor Adams.

As Trey dropped his eyes to the ground, he thought about it a little, then said, "Ever since we went to that show in Cody, it's like there's this video playing in my head about what Star and I are going to do in that kind of competition. I can't really put it into words yet, but I can see it as plain as I'm lookin' at you. I mean every detail, the program, the costume, the music, everything. Even the steps I'm gonna have to do in the training. I can't hardly sleep cuz I'm thinkin' 'bout it all the time!"

The pastor watched as Trey used his entire body to describe what he was feeling and as he finished the pastor let a smile slowly split his face, then said, "Yup, that's what I mean. When you just let yourself absorb everything that's coming your way, you will be able to shape it into a special meaning just for you."

The rest of the week was repetition after repetition of the same maneuvers with small adjustments and slight additions. After the duo finally coordinated on the sliding stop, Trey began to introduce the rollback and continued to work on the stop with the rear hooves sliding while the front legs walked

117

out the stop. The rollback is initiated after the stop is complete and is the action of the horse lifting his front quarters and turning around to go in the opposite direction. The days were spent on lead changes, sliding stops and rollbacks as both rider and horse honed their skills. The pastor visited twice more in the week and offered advice only when asked. The teacher and student continued the training of the mind regarding reading and comprehension. As with the training of the horse, the training of the boy was showing great progress.

Skye joined Trey again on Saturday and watched as Trey exhibited the progress they were making. When Trey joined her in the bleachers for a quick lunch, Skye said, "Hey guy, how about coming with me to church tomorrow. Pastor Adams would be happy to see you there. You know, he's been giving you a lot of his time and you haven't even come to church yet. How 'bout it, cowboy?"

Trey was sitting with his elbows on his knees as he held the sandwich in his hands. He turned his head to look at his friend to read her facial expression. Noting nothing mischievous or sinister, he turned his attention back to his sandwich, then said, "I ain't never been to church before. Whaddya do?"

"Well, we sing songs, listen to the pastor's message, then we go home. Nothin' complicated 'bout it."

"I don't know, I guess I could," he mumbled.

"Did you say yes?" exclaimed Skye as she slapped him on the shoulder.

"Not if you're gonna be beatin' on me. But, yeah, I guess I can come. You gonna give me a ride?"

"Course I will!" she said through her smile.

Chapter 19: Church

TREY DIDN'T KNOW what he expected, but it wasn't this. The parking lot had more pickups and horse trailers than cars, and the people going into the building were wearing jeans, boots and hats. The building was a large steel structure that was an indoor arena used by the locals for team roping and "cowboy" events. Today was the day for Cowboy Church. As they entered, the crowd was gathering on the bleachers and others had brought folding chairs they pulled up to the steel pipe fence. At the near end over the roping box, a platform had been placed on which a group of musicians were warming up in anticipation of the beginning of the service. A woman with a fringed denim skirt and matching vest, stood at a keyboard and played individual notes for the other musicians to tune their instruments. Two men had guitars, one an electric and one a standard with electric pickup, another man was tuning his upright bass while a young lady of about 14 tucked a fiddle under her chin and drew a bow across the strings. Seated behind the tuners, a young man with a string tie loosely hanging from his open collar shirt had his arms across his chest and held two drumsticks in one hand as he tapped his foot on the pedal for the bass drum.

No sooner had Trey and Skye and her mother taken their seats in the middle of the bleachers than the musicians struck up a lively tune that prompted a few of the crowd to clap their hands and tap their feet. On a screen near the band, the words to the music were projected and everyone started singing. The song was new to Trey but it certainly brought smiles to everyone around them. The second song was just as lively but the next song had a much slower tempo and more somber words, but Trey listened and enjoyed the music. At the conclusion of the third song, from the far end of the arena trotted a dapple grey with Pastor Adams on his customary Wade saddle.

The pastor greeted the crowd, made the usual welcoming comments then told about the coming events with a special invitation to the pot-luck picnic following services next Sunday. He then introduced the soloist for the day as Juanita Cortez who was also the fiddle player. The pastor backed his horse away from the railing and to the side of the crowd, focusing all attention on the band platform. When Juanita stepped to the front, the musicians began the introduction and she began to sing the old hymn, Amazing Grace. Although Trey had heard the song before, it was never by a young lady and definitely not with a cowboy band that gave it a country sound. She had a sweet voice and everyone enjoyed her rendition and showed their appreciation with applause.

As the pastor cued his horse to the front and center of the crowd, he laid his open Bible on the wide flat horn of the Wade saddle. He then began, "My text for this morning is found in the book of Ephesians, chapter 2, verses 8 and 9." While many in the crowd had Bibles in their laps and were busy turning to the assigned verses, Trey focused his attention on the pastor and his horse. He watched closely to see if he could pick up on the cues he used to control the movements of his mount. The horse sat in a docile manner while the pastor began his message and Skye nudged Trey to show him her open Bible and the verses the pastor was referencing. As Pastor Adams began making point after point, Trey noticed him give a slight leg cue or pressure that moved the horse to do a side pass along the rail. The horse did it so casually the average observer would not notice the easy side stepping motion as the horse would move the outside leg, then the inside leg next to it, and continue that motion as long as the leg pressure was applied. Usually when the horse and rider had progressed to one side of the crowd, they would then do just the opposite side pass across the front of the crowd to the other end and then back to the middle to rest a bit. All the while, the pastor didn't hesitate or indicate in any way that his attention was on anything but each and every member of the congregation. Then something the pastor said caught Trey's attention and he began to listen as the pastor spoke.

"Back in my youthful days of foolishness when I fancied myself a bull rider, in a rodeo down in Colorado I happened to draw a pretty rank bull by the name of Orange Crush. Now that bull was known not only for bucking all the cowboys off, but goin' after 'em after they were down and tryin' to pound them into the ground. Hence the name. Well, true to form, when I had my go, he bucked me off about 2 seconds before the whistle and it seemed like I was flyin' thru the air for those 2 long seconds. When I landed, I was unable to move, but I saw that crazy bull comin' at me with blood in his eyes. But just before he got to me, a figure flashed by me in front of that crazy bull. They used to call them rodeo clowns, but now they have the well deserved moniker of bull fighter. That's exactly what that funny attired fella did, as he went by he slapped that ol' bull on the face and took his attention off me and away they went. That fella dodged behind his barrel out there in the middle of the arena and kept that bull's attention while two other cowboys grabbed me and carried me out of there. And you see folks, that's what I mean by grace. I didn't deserve to get saved from that bull but he saved me anyway. What I did deserve for my foolishness was to get stomped into hell itself, but I didn't. That's what Jesus does for us by His grace. He rescues us when we don't deserve it and saves us from an eternity in hell. So, you ask, how do we get that grace? Well the rest of that verse says it's by faith. And faith is just takin' God at His word, or believing Him. 'For by grace are you saved through faith, and that not of yourselves, it is a gift from God, not of works, lest any man should boast.' So, my friend, if you want to be saved from that eternal hell, and you want to experience God's grace. Just take God at His word, believe in Him and ask Him to save you." With slightly applied leg pressure, his horse backed away from the fence, and with another unseen cue, his horse stretched his left front leg and tucked his right leg under his chest, then dropping his head, pastor and horse bowed in prayer.

As the pastor said, "Amen," the band started quietly playing as the people rose to leave. Several made their way down to the fence to speak with the pastor and with a head nod, Trey indicated to Skye they should go there as well. When the pastor was free, he stepped down from his horse and came to the rail to greet them, "Hey guys, it sure is great to see you. Especially you Trey. This is your first time here, isn't it?"

"This is my first time in any church."

"So, ya think ya might come back?" inquired the pastor.

"Oh, probably. I guess so," replied Trey noncommittally.

"Good, good. Say, I also have something to tell you. Wait around while I put up Smokey and I'll tell you all about it."

Skye and Trey returned to the bleachers where Skye's mother was visiting with one of her friends, and sat down to wait for the pastor's return. Within just a few minutes the pastor appeared as he put a foot on the second rail of the fence and threw his leg over the top and dropped to the ground in front of the bleachers. He walked over and sat down next to Trey and patted him on the shoulder saying, "Yessir, I'm sure glad to see you today. Let me tell you what I found out. You know the Lander Pioneer Days are coming up pretty soon, right?"

"Uh, yeah. So?" replied Trey with a quizzical look on his face. He had no idea what that annual celebration had to do with him, but he was willing to wait for the explanation.

"Well, this year, they're adding a few events to the rodeo and horse show. They've asked me to help them organize a reining horse competition and maybe even a Versatility competition as well, a lot like what we went to up in Cody," the broad smile on his face belied his excitement.

Trey looked at him carefully trying to see what he wasn't saying or at least what he was implying. "So, I take it by you're telling me this, you're thinking about Star and me getting' in it?

"That's exactly what I'm saying. I think it would be great experience for both of you."

"But isn't that coming up pretty soon?" questioned Trey.

"It will give you about two, two and a half weeks to get ready. Now, I don't think you need to go all out with a fancy costume and all that, but if you get the basics down and get comfortable with a program, I think you two could do pretty well."

"Do I have to give you an answer right now?" he asked with the fear showing in his voice.

"No, you've got plenty of time. You think about it, work together with Skye here to put together a program, and if it looks possible, then we can see about getting you entered," explained the pastor. His enthusiasm showed his optimism and that was an encouragement to Trey. Trey thought, *He actually thinks we can do it. I wonder, maybe.*

Star Dancer

Chapter 20: Preparation

THE KITCHEN TABLE was cluttered with paper used for diagrams, printed copies of the rules for the Free Style reining competition, and sketches of possible costumes. Trey was standing at the counter behind Skye and pouring a glass of iced tea for each of them. Skye was resting her head on one open palm while the other hand hung on to a pencil that seemed to have a mind of its own as a diagram of a possible performance was taking shape. Her elbow was the prop for the hand on her head, and she had one leg tucked under the other while the free leg stretched to a bare foot swinging under the table. With her sketching hand and her bare foot moving in a rhythmic cadence, she blurted, "I've got it! This is the one!"

The shouted alarm brought Trey to her side as he leaned over her shoulder to see the newly drawn diagram. Skye began to explain, "You come into the arena from here," as she pointed to the drawing, "and at a canter go straight to the judges stand with a sliding stop. Then do the two spins, and come out of your spins into the large figure eight to make one and a half turns on the eight, that'll give your two lead changes. Then come out of the eight at a full canter to the left end of the arena for a full stop. Do a roll back and go to the other end with another slider, back up out of that to a stop. Then the rest will be whatever else you want to do for free style. The required maneuvers will only take about half your time, and you can then have as much time as you want for the rest. That'll work, won't it?" She said as she turned to face him, bringing her face within an inch or two of his. He was looking down at her with a somber expression as he seemed to be looking deep into her eyes and her spirit. Neither one moved or even breathed, but each seemed to savor the moment of closeness as they waited breathlessly. The ice cubes in the tea glass tumbled upon one another and broke the stillness. Trey looked down. "Uh, yeah. Sounds great," he managed, as he made his way to the chair at the end of the small table.

He pulled the diagram in front of him, followed the lines and arrows with his fingers, and said, "I see what you mean. This will work great. Most of those we saw up in Cody came out and did the circles and lead changes first. This jumps right out at the judges and kinda makes 'em pay attention. I like it. Course, I gotta get Star to agree with me. We got a lotta work to do."

With her usual mischievous smile Skye looked at him with a sidelong smirk and said, "And what were you thinkin' 'bout a costume?"

"Well, I can tell you've already got something up your sleeve. So, out with it."

"So, I was thinkin' how 'bout a costume like many use at the Sun Dance?" she shared. Skye was one of the best dancers on the reservation and usually took top honors at the pow wows with both her dancing and her costume. Trey knew she wanted to be involved in this part of his performance and he also knew that whatever she did would be extraordinary.

"Well, we're thinking along the same lines. But, whatever you do, I want you to include my grandmother and her friends. I really want to include her in all this."

"Are you kidding? Of course I would. Your grandmother and her circle have always been known as some of the best

126

when it comes to putting together a costume. Their skill with beadwork and leather work is unbelievable. I would be thrilled to work with them," Skye replied. The two friends left the kitchen and started to the corral and tack shed, when Trey turned to Skye and said, "There's something else," and he began to share with her what he had envisioned for his ultimate performance, what he had imagined and dreamed. It was a sharing unlike anything he had done before, as this came from the hidden depths that he had harbored protectively and was unwilling to let anyone see that part of his spirit. As he finished, he put one foot up on the bottom rail of the fence, an arm over the top rail and he looked at the cloudless sky and said, "But that's not for now. But I thought if you knew about it, what you do now could be a beginning of that. Do you understand what I mean."

Skye slipped her hand in his and looked up to see him turn toward her. "Yes. I understand. And, Trey, thanks for letting me see that with you."

With nothing more than a deep breath and exhale, he turned to the tack shed to get the gear for his horses and to prepare for the day's training. While he saddled Pepper and brought Star out of the corral with the halter and lead rope, Skye returned to the kitchen to retrieve the program plan sketch and drawings. She went out the front door as Trey led both horses around the side of the house to join her and Praline at the front. Trey's mom joined then on the front step as she asked, "Are you gonna be trainin' most of the day at the arena?"

"Yeah, but I'll be home, oh, late afternoon. I don't wanna wear him out. He'll probably wear me out, though."

With a smile his mom replied, "O.K. I'll be leavin' for work pretty soon, so if you're not up when I get home. I'll see you in the mornin'. Skye, you take care of him, now."

"O.K. But as you know, that can be a full time job!" Skye replied.

Trey rolled his eyes at his friend as he said, "So, now you're gangin' up on me?" Turning to his mom he said, "All right

Mom. Have a good night." Then mounting up he turned back to her with, "Love ya." She echoed his sentiment as she returned into the house.

Three horses, two teenagers and one dog made a small procession in the direction of the work-out arena, kicking up the powdery dust of the roadway with their shuffling gait. Trey was thinking about the program, the individual exercises, and the training that would be necessary. Skye was used to his extended periods of silence as she knew him well enough to know that his retreating into himself was not a reflection on her but simply his newly discovered way of free thinking. With the exercise diagram rolled up, she used it as a wake-up baton and slapped his arm to get his attention. "Hey, what time did you say Jeremy was gonna come and put shoes on Star?" referring to the slider shoes recommended by pastor Adams. Trey had called Jeremy Thacker, the farrier, and asked him to come out and do the horseshoeing. Jeremy was kind of a 'Jack of all trades' man that did a little horse training, horseshoeing, and also had a nice little ranch just West of town. He had a forge, anvil and all the necessary tools to take care of the job.

"He said he should be able to get here shortly after lunch. Why?"

"I was thinkin' 'bout goin' to see your grandmother and talk to her about the costume. She's gonna wanna get started right away, I'm sure. So, after lunch, I think I'll go see her. Ya think that'll be alright?" she inquired.

"I'm sure she'll be tickled pink to see you and to get involved."

Arriving at the arena, Trey followed the usual routine of unsaddling Pepper and turning him loose in one of the holding pens along with Skye's Praline, while Tobey supervised. He had never put even a blanket on Star and only used a bosal for any training or control. Switching the halter for the bosal, he draped the halter on the fence post by the gate to the holding pen. Tobey took off on his usual scouting expedition to see if there had been any visitors since the last time he was here.

Leading Star to the middle of the long rail fence opposite the announcers booth, he did his customary hop and belly straddle to mount his stallion. Skye had climbed to the announcer's booth for a 'bird's eye view' of the day's events. Letting the mecate rein rest on Star's neck, Trey used his leg pressure and hand touches to maneuver the horse into position. Before and during any requested movement, Trey always communicated verbally and physically with Star.

The beginning of every training day was spent in review of the previously taught exercises and maneuvers. Trey began with his usual walk-through, then picked up the pace with a trot into the larger circles of the figure eight as they worked on the lead changes. Star seemed to intuitively know what was expected and executed the maneuver flawlessly. In the previous days, Trey had just begun to introduce Star to the spin maneuver and now used the bosal to start him in the spin movement. The leg cue required pressure on the outside of the turn but the momentum of the spin made the maintaining of the pressure difficult. Especially since Trey was not on a saddle and had only his hand pressure on the inside of the withers to counter the momentum to the outside. This was made very real to Trey as he once again found himself on the ground looking up at Star. *Well, boy, I guess I'm gonna have to work on that some more ain't I?* It was then he heard the voice from the announcer's stand, "And coming out of chute number three, it's Trey Standingelk on the mustang Star. Oops, not on Star anymore. I guess that's what you call a shooting star!" The one person applause was barely heard over so much laughter from such a small girl.

Trey's second, third, and fourth effort at executing the spin all went much better. By the fifth try, it appeared Star was beginning to understand the anchoring of his inside rear hoof and using his front legs to work the spin. With minimal effort, he readily increased his speed in the execution of the spin. Trey had mastered the settling of his weight and his leg pressure. The main concern was if both horse and rider could repeat their success going the other direction. However, with repeated tries, the spin was executed in both directions, although not flawless enough for a performance.

Skye had packed the lunch and now spread a blanket on one of the benches of the bleachers and laid out the noon fare. Trey was glad to join her on a seat that was a little more stationary than what he had been trying to stay on aboard Star. With the type of canned heat used for camping, she warmed up a helping of aluminum-foil wrapped prepared meat. A plastic container held a mixture of lettuce, tomatoe, cheese, and avocadoes, and a second aluminum foil package was opened to reveal two oval shaped pieces of fried bread. Putting the bread on the paper plates, Skye then spooned the meat directly onto the bread and buried it under a generous helping of the salad mixings. Adding a little bit of hot sauce and sour cream, she put a plastic fork and knife on the side and presented the offering to Trey. His wide eyes, face splitting smile, and eager reach told Skye he was impressed. *Mission accomplished,* she thought with a smile of her own.

"Wow, this sure beats that venison summer sausage and crackers!" he said.

"Yeah, I was kinda gettin' burnt out on them," Skye replied.

After finishing lunch and packing everything away in the shoulder bag, Skye started to the holding pen to saddle up Praline. Trey walked with her and reached down to take the bag, then dropped his hand to hers to hold her hand as they walked. He opened the gate and entered the pen, catching Praline by her halter, then led her to the fence to saddle her for Skye. She had just mounted up when they heard the approaching vehicle and turned to see the familiar pickup of the farrier.

"Tell Grandmother I said hi and thank her for me, O.K.?"

"You know I will. I'll either come by or call you at home, depending on the time," she said as she gigged Praline toward the road.

With a wave to Skye, Trey turned to greet Jeremy and ready Star for the horseshoeing. In just shy of two hours, the job was done. As he was packing up his equipment, Jeremy said, "How 'bout walking him around a little bit. Then maybe a canter and maybe even a sliding stop so we can see how he takes to his new shoes?"

Trey was happy to oblige and did a walk-around the familiar figure eight pattern, then kicked star up to a canter for the same pattern as Star did the lead changes perfectly. As they came out of the far circle, he cued Star into a full run toward the end of the arena and executed a sliding stop with Star's hind quarters dropping and his tail dragging behind him and his hind legs and hooves digging flawless parallel furrows. Jeremy responded with, "I don't know which is more impressive, the smoothness of your horse's moves, or the fact you were able to stay on him during that slide." Trey smiled broadly knowing that was high praise from the horse trainer.

Calling it a day, Trey saddled Pepper, whistled for Tobey and leading Star the trio headed for home. Trey was surprised to see his mom's car in the driveway as her work schedule usually called for her to be at work at this time of day. It was late afternoon as he walked his horses up the driveway and around the house to put them up for the night in their corral. He put the saddle in the tack room on the rack, hung up the bridle, bosal, and halters, gave them some hay, and started for the house. His mom was waiting at the kitchen door with a somber look on her face. *Either I'm in trouble or there's something bad wrong,* thought Trey. "What is it, Mom. What's wrong?" he asked as he stepped up to the doorway. He could tell his mom was upset and had been crying. "Oh, honey. We've got to go. Your dad's work called, he's been hurt and they're taking him to the hospital. We need to get there right away."

Star Dancer

Chapter 21: Hospital

TREY AND HIS MOM were the only ones not attired in hospital scrubs. The many green workers reminded Trey of the ant hill in their back yard, everybody in a hurry and looking important yet it seemed like nobody was in charge. Green people going up the hall, green people going down the hall, some carrying armloads of paraphernalia and others pushing machines or poles with tubes and plastic containers. Even with the hustle and bustle, the overriding sensation was the smell of antiseptics and floor wax. *Just another reason why I like the mountains better* thought Trey as he followed his mom through the maze of hallways and signs. Pushing her way through a pair of swinging doors, the two entered the emergency room corridor and were greeted by a woman in a colorful top and matching cap covered with multi-colored balloons. "May I help you Mam?" she questioned, making it a point to stand in the middle of the corridor and block their way.

"I'm looking for my husband, Stoney Standingelk, he was brought in from his work," she stated questioning and looking for a positive answer.

"Oh, yes, he's over here in bed three. You can go over there and see him, but he might be a little drowsy, we just gave him a sedative," she informed them as she stepped aside and motioned to the far curtain. It was apparent there was an immediate conflict between the nurse and Trey's mom, and turning away, they quickly headed for the prescribed bed to see Stoney. Stepping to the side of the bed, Sophie bent close to Stoney's face and whispered, "Stoney, honey, it's Sophie and Trey."

As he turned to face her his eyes fluttered open and a smile creased his weathered face, as he responded, "Hey babe," he moved his hand to rest on hers on the top of the side rail. Trey remained at the foot of the bed and did not intervene in the lover's reunion. "Have they told you what happened? And what they're gonna do?"

"Nobody's told us anything. So, what did happen?"

"Ah, we were swingin' in some more drill pipe and one broke loose and chased me off the rig. As you might have figgered, I lost that race. Coulda been worse though," he grunted.

"So, what'd ya hurt?" she asked hesitatingly.

"Well, I got a few cuts and bruises from hittin' the ground, but the worst of it is the end of that pipe took out my leg. They're gonna operate on it and put it back together. Guess it's broke up pretty bad, but they say I should come out O.K."

Taking a deep breath, she asked, "What do they mean, O.K.?"

"They won't know for sure until after they get in there, but I'll probably be off work for two or three months."

The drop of her shoulders revealed the release of tension as she turned and found the chair. Pulling it beside the bed, she said, "When I got the call they didn't tell me anything. I was expecting the worst, so it's good to know it's only a leg."

Looking to the foot of the bed to see his son, he said, "Would ya listen ta her? Only a leg! But it's my leg, and it ain't like I got a few ta spare." He smiled as he winked at his son. There had never been a close relationship between father and son with work and school schedules taking the blame, but it was really a blend of culture, environment and personality. In any culture, the father that takes the time to be a father shows his children his respect for them and the relationship with the priority he places on that time. When Trey was still a toddler, Stoney had invested more time with his son, taking him fishing and on other outings. But as the boy grew Stoney's insecurity with fatherhood made it easy to focus on work instead of family.

A nurse and an orderly interrupted the reunion as they pushed the curtain aside and the nurse said, "O.K. folks, we're gonna take him down the hall to the O.R. There's a waiting room just outside the O.R. and you can wait there for word from the doctor."

Sophie directed her question to the matronly looking nurse, "How long do you think it'll be," as she stepped around the end of the bed.

"Probably around an hour or two, but the doctor will talk to you before he starts."

With a dismissive gesture, she bent to unlock the wheels on the bed and re-adjust the I.V. pole and apparatus. Trey and his mom stepped aside and turned to go to the waiting room. No sooner had they claimed their seats and reached for a magazine, and the doctor walked in and came directly to speak with them. "Are you the family of Stoney?" he inquired, although there was no one else in the waiting room. After receiving an affirmative reply, he proceeded to tell them what he expected to do and how long it would take, but that a nurse would be in to give them updates on the progress. He even suggested trying the cafeteria for some coffee or other refreshment.

Every magazine was dog eared and out-of-date but they shuffled through them in a vain attempt to occupy their minds and consume the time. Trey stood and walked to the hallway and paced the length and back. Turning back into the waiting room, he went to his chosen chair and flopped down with a heavy sigh. His mom watched him as he showed his frustration. "Why is it that these places have the most uncomfortable chairs in the world. What do they do, shop for them in the uncomfortable chair store?"

"A little frustrated are you?" she asked with a slight smile tugging at her face. "I'm sure your father is going to be all right, but it'll take time. We will have to help him all we can, cuz it's gonna be different and it's gonna take time."

"Mom, I wanna help, but he really hasn't had a lot to do with me recently. And, I made a commitment to do that horse show with Star and that takes a lotta time too. I don't wanna sound selfish, but what are we gonna do? Will he even want my help? And what can I do?"

Reaching her hand to touch his arm in a display of reassurance, she said, "We'll just have to take it one step at a time. I know your dad hasn't been real involved with you lately, but he asks about you and your horse. He is interested, I think he just doesn't know how to show it. All his time is spent with the big tough macho oil rig workers and none of them willing to show emotion or don't know how, and then they come home to a family and they're at a loss as to what to do. But I think if we just take it one day at a time, we can help each other. Maybe this time will be good for our family."

The ride home seemed longer than usual. Trey was deep in thought about his dad and what the days ahead would involve. The doctor had told them they should be able to take him home tomorrow, but it was going to be difficult for a while. The cast went from his hip to his toes on his right leg and it would be a while before his dad would be able to get around even with crutches. He would need help with just about everything and that would take a lot of time. His thoughts were interrupted by his mom saying, "I think I'm gonna take some time off work. Maybe even a month. Yeah, that should do it. A good month of stayin' at home with my family. Maybe even longer. Whadda ya think Trey? Could you use some good home cooked meals?"

He turned to look at his mom and thought about what she said, then he realized it was as much for him as it was for his dad. With his mom at home, he would be free to work with Star and could probably even make it to the horse show and the Free Style competition. With that one short conversation, his face brightened up and he responded, "Wow. That sounds great mom. Thanks!"

Chapter 22: Together

THE MORNING WAS SPENT getting Stoney settled in at home. They made the couch his new temporary bed so he would be in the center of any activity and wouldn't feel locked away in a back bedroom. Setting up a side table with his pain meds and bandages for his few minor cuts, they also made room for his coffee and snack tray. His bedside accessory was made complete with the TV remote and the wireless phone receiver. The rest of the living room furniture was rearranged for the convenience of the invalid and his wheelchair, walker and crutches. Although he wasn't able to use any of these, he wanted them nearby for whenever he was game enough to give them a trial run. After Stoney was situated, Sophie turned to the kitchen and her preparations for the family meals. She put a pork roast in the crock pot and made out a list for the groceries they would need with everyone eating three meals at home.

After assembling a ham sandwich and grabbing a bottle of water, Trey said to his mom, "Skye is going to meet me at the arena a little later. Right now she's over at Grandmother's and they're conspiring together about my costume for the Free Stlyle. So, if it's alright, I'm gonna head out with Star and

Pepper and go get some training in at the arena." He was used to it just being him and his mom and had neglected to talk to his dad about his plans. Now from the other room, he heard his father call to him.

"Hey, come here a minute, Trey."

As he walked into the other room and faced the figure that vaguely resembled his father, it was different to look down on him instead of the usual looking up to the imposing figure of his broad shouldered and husky six foot plus father. He was set at ease with a broad smile from his dad as he said, "So, tell me about this horse and the progress you've been making. I wanna hear it all."

Trey took a seat on the nearby chair his mother had arranged for the two of them and started with the show he had seen in Cody. After concluding with the pastor's suggestion of the Lander Pioneer Days competition and the training thus far, he said, "So, that's about it. We've only got about another week and a half, and a lot more work to do on his maneuvers. Skye and Grandmother and her friends are working on a costume, so we're hoping it'll all come together."

With an arm stretched across the top of the back of the couch, his dad looked at his son with a new found respect. "And you've done all that just since you caught that horse, when?"

"Dad, that was clear back in the Spring. I've been working with him almost every day. He is amazing and we just seem to click together. Pastor Adams said he's never seen anyone with that kind of connection before."

"And this pastor Adams, what would he know about horses?" asked his dad.

"He's the pastor at the Cowboy Church and he used to be a rodeo hand and he's done quite a bit of horse training. You should see his horse when he's preaching," stated Trey.

"Doesn't sound like any preacher I ever heard of, but sounds like he knows what he's doin' all right. Well, as soon as

I can get around, I wanna come out and see ya work. Would that be O.K.?

Scooting to the edge of the seat and grinning broadly at his dad, he replied, "O.K.? Of course. It would be great to have you give me some pointers. Sure. Hey mom, ya hear that? Dad wants to come out and see Star. Man, this is turning into a family thing. Great!" Stuffing the rest of his sandwich into his mouth and heading out the door, he crowded a "Good bye" past the remnants of the sandwich. He then mumbled a "See ya later!" before heading to the corral.

Skye was waiting for him at the arena and had tethered Praline to the top rail of the fence by the roping chute and the entry gate to the arena. As Trey neared with Pepper and Star, she asked, "How's your Dad?" as she walked to open the gate for the training trio.

"He's doin' O.K. but it's gonna take some time 'fore he gets up an' aroun'"

"Are you still gonna be able to do the Free Style?" she asked.

"Yeah. He even wants to come out as soon as he's able and see Star work," he informed her with a broad smile. Skye knew Trey was anxious to connect with his dad as that closeness had been missing in his life for some time. She was happy for him and she was also excited for the rest of the family to see the costume that she and his grandmother were putting together for him.

"That's great Trey. It'll be good to see him and I know he's gonna be impressed with you and Star. I can't wait till the Pioneer Days. And you're gonna like what your grandmother and I are making for your costume. Which, by the way, I'm gonna have to go help her this afternoon, so I'm not staying here very long. You really don't need me do you? You can fall off all by yourself," she snickered and smiled up at him.

"Fall off! I was just doin' that for your entertainment. And since you won't be here, I won't have to even get dirty!"

141

"All right, cowboy. I'm outta here on that one," she said as she closed the gate and turned to mount her little mare. "Call me tonite!" she instructed as she clucked her horse to a trot and waved at him over her shoulder.

Trey renewed his training routine with a walk through of each of the exercises. Then without following the planned program, he chose to just work on the individual exercises. Both he and Star needed to improve on the two more impressive ones, the sliding stop and the spin. Now he chose to begin with the spin and walked Star to the center of the arena. Although he had put the bosal on the stallion, he continued to work on the maneuvers using only pressure cues, shifting of his weight and the spoken command. His goal was to do the entire program without using the bosal or any other tack. It wasn't because he wanted to impress anyone as much as he just wanted Star to work with him without any forced movements prompted by the pressure of a bosal or bridle and bit. He hadn't even considered using a saddle or any similar accouterment due to his desire to be as close to the historic traditional way of his ancestors and the way they mastered the horse.

Mastering the sliding stop required as much if not more from Trey than Star. All Star had to do was lock his hind legs, drop his rear end, and walk it out with the front legs. Trey had to stay aboard this rapidly moving and quick stopping animal that resembled a contortionist and all without anything to hold onto except a short hank of mane at Star's withers. It took every muscle in his legs, his rear end, and the rest of his body to maintain his balance and not repeat his flying maneuver over Star's head. The repeated practice was showing its worth for both mount and rider. After plowing furrows all over the arena, he decided to take a break and get a drink and reward Star with a good long drink as well. The two walked to the holding pen and the full water tank just inside the gate. As Star drank his fill, Trey slipped the water bottle from his bottle pouch at his saddle that now sat on the top rail of the pen. As he tipped up the bottle, he saw the pastor's jeep coming into the arena drive.

He pulled the jeep alongside the rail fence at the holding pen and waited as Trey walked to greet him. The usual greetings exchanged, the pastor then said, "Say, I got to thinkin' bout you and Star and with his mustang lifestyle, it might be a good thing to get him used to other horses, crowds, people, and noise. You know, so he won't get spooked in the arena competition. Oh, and also, you need to get him trained to load into a horse trailer. That is, unless you're planning on riding him all the way to the arena in Lander."

As he leaned his forearms on the fence rail, he looked at the pastor and said, "I hadn't thought of that. I sure don't want to get him in the arena and have a one-man rodeo. That's for sure. I'm thinkin' you didn't come out here without havin' and idea on how to fix that. Am I right?"

"Yeah. Here's what I'm thinkin.' There's a ropin' here at the arena Thursday night. Why don't you come out early, have Star in a holdin' pen to begin with, and then ride him around a little with the rest of the horses and the people in the grandstands, just to get him used to it. That way it'll be kinda gradual and he should be able to handle it. If you like, I'll bring out my trailer and park it here and you can use it when you want to get him used to loadin' an' unloadin'. How's that sound?"

"That's be great, pastor, thanks! I'll plan on that."

"By the way. I heard about your dad. How's he doin'? Is there anything I can do or anything you need?" inquired the pastor.

Trey was a little surprised at the pastor's concern and offer. He didn't know Trey's dad or mom, but he seemed genuinely concerned and sincerely offered to help. Trey was not only surprised, but pleased as well. "He's doin' pretty good. It's gonna take a while, but we're doin' all right. Thanks."

"Well, I'd like to meet your folks sometime. But for now, I gotta run. I'll bring out that trailer as soon as I can. In the meantime, keep up the good work," he said as he started his jeep and pulled away.

Chapter 23: Crowds

WHEN GRANDMOTHER SAYS, "I need you to come here," the only acceptable response is "I'll be right over." It doesn't matter if you're the son, grandson, nephew or other relative or not, Grandmother is a term used for the elder women and much respect is given by everyone. In this case, she was Trey's Grandmother and she expected Trey to come for a fitting of his costume for the Free Style competition. Although many of the contestants of the competition wore costumes, it was not mandatory and of all those normally seen, most were worn by the women contestants and consisted of lots of flowing material to accent the movement of the horse. The few costumes worn by men were more conservative and much less impressive. When Skye began her design of a costume for Trey, she did not allow herself to be hindered or restricted by other's expectations. Knowing Trey had a particular desire to honor his ancestors and the ancient ways, her design resembled the many costumes made for the different dances of the pow-wows. Today would be the first time Trey was to see and be fitted for parts of the costume.

Grandmother had solicited the help of two of her lifelong friends, Mary Cloud Walker and Jane Blackstone, they had often worked together with many different crafts and most often making dance costumes. Mary's specialty was intricate beadwork, Jane's particular skill was seen with leatherwork, and Grandmother Standingelk excelled with feathers. Every part of a costume used many different skills and all worked together on Skye's design. Skye was thrilled and honored to be able to work with these women that were held in such high esteem by everyone that knew of their skill. It was truly a learning experience that she would cherish.

When Trey arrived he was welcomed with broad smiles and greetings from all and a special lingering hug from his Grandmother. When she pulled back to look at her grandson, she said, "I am so proud of you and we are so excited to see you compete with your wild mustang. This is going to be a first for our people and we are honored to be a part." Both Mary and Jane were smiling and nodding their heads in agreement as they sat around the cluttered kitchen table. As Trey looked around the modest home, it seemed there were feathers, beads, and leather on almost every flat surface. Skye served as his guide as she pulled him to the living room and reached for a pair of fringed leggings. The deep gold buckskin leather leggings were fringed all the way down the side of each leg with fringe about six inches long. The leather was so soft the first reaction was to stroke his hand down the smooth leg. Skye instructed him to go into the bedroom and put them on and come out to be fitted. She also handed him a matching vest and a pair of moccasins.

He stood in the middle of the archway between the kitchen and the living room for a few moments, before the busy women looked up to see him. Conversation stopped as each one looked at the young man who was an image of an ancient warrior. The vest, leggings and moccasins were all plain, but seemed to fit pretty well, as far as Trey was concerned. But the ladies immediately surrounded him and touched and pulled on various points, made a few light marks for alterations and placement of beadwork, and commented to one another all the while. Their excitement was contagious and a big smile spread on Trey's face as he looked over the matronly trio to see Skye stifling a silent laugh at his seeming embarrassment.

After returning the leather basics to the ladies to resume their creative work, Skye pulled him aside to show him her sketch of his costume. She had used colored pencils and her artwork was exceptional. Trey was amazed at what she had created and even more amazed when he realized what was being created just for him. Looking down at Skye he said, "Wow. This is beautiful. Is it going to be just like this?"

"Yes, silly. Of course. What is so special is what these ladies can do. This is going to be something that will last your lifetime."

Trey was at a loss for words, but the water that welled in his lower eyelids said all she needed to hear. "Now, get outta here and go work with Star. And by the way, I'm gonna work on him too," she declared as she shut the door behind him.

Although the training day was cut short with the visit to Grandmother's, it was still going to be a long day. Tonight was the night of the team roping at the arena and the time for Star to get acquainted with a busy arena and crowds of both horses and people. Pastor Adams drove into the arena area with his goose neck horse trailer behind his Chevy pickup and parked it in the area to the North of the arena where most activity participants parked their trailers. His was the first to arrive and Trey would have the rest of the afternoon to work on the loading and unloading with Star. The pastor stopped the pickup, stepped out and started to unhitch the trailer as Trey joined him to help. "Hi Trey. Here ya go! This is a three horse slant, double doors at the back and a walk out door here near the front. Have you ever loaded a horse in one like this?"

"A few times. Last huntin' season, I went with Uncle Chico and we used a trailer like this. Course, Pepper is an old hand at loadin' so I didn't think much of it at the time," responded Trey as he looked over the trailer.

"Then mebbe whatcha need ta do is load Pepper first and Star won't be so spooked at the idea. Also, keep this front door open so it won't look like a dead end for 'em," advised pastor Adams. "I'll leave it here, I've got a couple a calls I gotta make, but I'll be back this evenin' cuz I wanna see how he does around crowds. I'm sure he'll be O.K., just take your time with him."

The pastor climbed back in the cab of his pickup and with an arm out the window opening, he turned back to Trey and asked, "As I pull out, put that tailgate up for me, O.K.?" He pulled forward about six feet, stopped while Trey put the tailgate up and waved, then pulled out to the exit of the arena grounds. Trey walked to the holding pen where the two horses stood with heads over the top rail watching all the new activity and awaiting Trey's return, hoping for a treat. He didn't disappoint them.

Leading the two horses out of the holding pen and to the trailer, Trey first tied off Star's lead to one of the tie rings on the side of the trailer. He had previously opened both the side door and the rear loading doors and now led Pepper to the rear to load him up into the trailer. Without hesitation, Pepper followed Trey into the trailer. The unit was white outside and had been white on the inside but had been redecorated by its many previous occupants with their recycled feed. He tied Pepper off by the open window with the gelding's head by the window bars making him visible to Star standing tied to that side of the trailer. Exiting out the front side door, Trey untied Star and led him to the rear of the trailer. Taking his time and slowly acquainting the stallion with this new contraption, he let the horse investigate by looking it over, sniffing it thoroughly and mumbling a low throaty question to his corral companion. Trey stepped up into the trailer, gave a slight tug on the lead rope, then extended his free hand with an apple treat. It seemed whenever Star focused on an apple treat, he lost all awareness of what else was happening and as Trey stepped back, Star stepped up into the trailer in pursuit of the treat. With a couple more steps, the stallion was completely in the trailer. Trey tied him off at the tie ring next to the divider, stepped under Pepper's neck and exited the trailer. He shut the doors, walked to the windows and spoke to his horses. Then went to the rear door, opened it and proceeded to unload the two horses. He repeated this complete action three more times, each without incident and the last two times without bribery, giving Trey a sense of satisfaction and pride in his red horse.

The next few hours were spent with the usual routine of walk-thru reviews of the different exercises, then more concentrated working on the more complex maneuvers. Both horse and rider were getting more comfortable with each maneuver and were also gaining confidence in the overall program. Usually the last thing the pair did before the conclusion of each day's practice was to do a complete run thru of the entire program as it had to become a natural progression to be completed without the thinking and pondering of the next exercise. As the confidence increased, the program became smoother in each transition, and the more natural it felt for both horse and rider. After the completion of the program, the two stood still and savored the moment as Trey would lay down on the neck of Star and with both arms hug, pat and stroke the neck of his best friend as a reward to both.

Trey was sitting on the top rail of the holding pen and watched the many participants and observers as they came into the arena. The grandstand bleachers were beginning to fill up, mostly with family members of the ropers and friends. The pastor's trailer had disappeared in the crowd of trailers, many similar in appearance. Many ropers were limbering up their mounts as they rode around the arena, usually swinging ropes over their heads to reacquaint their mounts with the purpose for their visit to the arena. The larger holding pen between the one where Trey's horses were and the roping boxes was filled with the many steers to be used in the planned event. All had protective rubber from inner tubes around their horns to prevent injury from the cowboy's ropes. Trey dropped into the pen with Star, hooked the lead rope to his halter and led him to the gate to introduce him to the organized pandemonium of people and animals.

Not knowing what to expect and with his heart trying to beat its way out of his chest, Trey had a looped grip on the lead rope as the two exited the holding pen. Star had his head held high and he pranced with excitement and watched the activity around him. Eyes wide and white, emitting an occasional whinney of question, he often twisted his head around to see what was behind him and forward again so as not to miss anything. Trey knew Star had been raised in a herd of mustangs so the many horses were nothing new, but with each one carrying a rider and some walking together, some trotting and stopping, others a full canter around the perimeter of the arena, the activity must have been slightly alarming. A factor Trey had overlooked was the simple fact that Star was a stallion and many of these horses were mares. That alone added to the tension between the many animals. The arena never seemed so big as they walked around the perimeter, nearing the roping boxes and the end of the journey, Star was startled by one of the ropers coming up behind them and throwing a rope at his heels as if he was a steer and the roper was a heeler. The touch of the rope caused Star to immediately buck and kick back at the horse and rider, barely missing the head of the horse.

"Hey, you better get control of that horse boy!" shouted the perpetrator of Star's action.

Trey quickly responded, "If you don't know the difference between a horse and a steer, maybe you better load up and go home!"

The cowboy immediately jumped from his horse and strode toward Trey with the idea of showing the kid what he was in for when two other cowboys rode their horses between Trey and the man. "Back off Jackson! You were wrong now quit making a fool of yourself and get back on your horse. Any more nonsense like that and you can leave!" warned the older man mounted on a tall black. Trey was to find out later that Jackson was one of the Blackman family and a known trouble maker, while the man that intervened was the organizer of the roping and the owner of the provided stock.

After the little dust up, Trey saddled up Pepper and leading Star the trio headed home. Although Tobey had been with him, he had made himself scarce most of the day but quickly appeared on the road beside his friends and trotted to the lead to point the way home. Although the pastor had said he would return, apparently he had been detained for some reason and Trey knew he would see him again in the coming days. If not at the arena, he would see him at church on Sunday. Church had become a regular on his schedule and he always enjoyed being with Skye and hearing the message. He was always amazed at the similarity in the beliefs of the native Arapaho and the Christian community. He supposed a lot of that was because the Arapaho had integrated the practices of the white man and his religion with theirs for well over one hundred years.

Star Dancer

Chapter 24: Rehearsal

AS TREY LIFTED his foot into the leg of the buckskin
leggings part of his competition attire, his hands felt the
softness of the golden tanned deer hide and his eyes continued
to take in the beauty of the beadwork that highlighted the front
thigh part of the pants. Now standing he ran his hands down
the fringe that decorated the sides of both legs and again
marveled at the softness. The snug fit felt good as he bent to
pull on the beaded moccasins and admired the continued
pattern of beadwork on the top of the foot ware. Noting the
detail of the descending eagle with outstretched wings that
covered the back and with smaller figures the front of the
matching vest, he slipped the work of art up to his shoulders as
the fringe draped over his bare shoulders and down the side.
He dropped the hairpipe and bead breast plate over his head
and picked up the beaded belt from the edge of the bed.
Wrapping the long leather belt around his waist, he tied it in
front and allowed the beaded portion to hand almost to his
knees. . Next came the breech cloth with the same eagle figure
and fringe as he pulled it up behind the belt and let it hang over
the front to display the large beaded area. The leather cuffs,
also fringed, were then fastened around his wrists with a

Velcro strip and allowed the cuffs to flare out and show the beadwork. He tried to get a complete view of himself in the small mirror above the dresser, but was unable to see anything but the upper portion of his body. He turned to walk to the living room and the awaiting group of artisans.

The three women and Skye collectively drew breath and began to comment on the impressive costume. His Grandmother motioned for him to be seated at the table. She stepped behind him and began by strapping a beaded headband around his head with a beaded circle to the front, then placed the double roach headpiece on his head and pulled the elastic strap beneath his chin. With one last adjustment, she motioned for him to stand and back away toward the front door. Nodding heads and muttered comments accompanied his brief movement. As he turned to face the ladies, grandmother Mary said, "You know, if I was about thirty years younger . . . " and a laugh from her two fellow artisans expressed their doubts that thirty years would be enough.

"Grandmother, this is so beautiful. I'm almost afraid to wear it."

Her startled expression spoke louder than her words as she said, "You think we worked this hard for that to hang in a closet? You wear it and you wear it with pride. When you put that on, we go with you and wherever you go and whatever you do, we are there with you. Don't ever forget that!" she admonished. A big smile tried to hide the gathering tears as she spread her arms wide to envelope her grandson. A tug at his arm revealed the other two ladies, also to be referred to as grandmother, wanting to join in the hug. Skye was seated on the small couch but was smiling with a special pride in her friend as well as her costume design.

Trey had always had the highest respect for his Grandmother and honored the traditions of his people. As he thought of the many hours and work of love shown in this costume, he tried to express his appreciation, yet before he spoke he knew he would fall short of truly expressing what was deep within him. As he looked at the wrinkled and weathered features, the crowns of white hair, and the eyes of wisdom, he was transported to the past and the time of the ancients. He saw himself in the village of warriors and proud families with children playing and women preparing meals over open fires while men attended the herds of horses and returned from extended hunts. And he spoke, "Grandmothers, I am honored by your skill and the work you've done. You make me proud to be Arapaho and I will do all I can to bring honor to you as you have honored me." He knelt on one knee and bowed his head in reverence before them.

Standing and turning to go to the bedroom, he stepped quickly through the door. He removed the headpieces and the cuffs, placed them in the tissue paper and boxes, then picking up his clothes and the boxes he returned to leave. "I needta work with Star Dancer with these on so he won't get spooked during the show. I'm gonna go through my entire routine later this afternoon if you ladies would like to come and see. My father and mother will see Star and me for the first time today." Without awaiting a reply, he dropped his head and left.

Star was unimpressed with his attire and showed no reaction whatever. As Trey thought about it, he realized his horse didn't really care what he wore. But being a bit cautious, he waited until he tethered Star to the arena fence and was watching Trey, before he donned the headband, double roach headpiece, and the fringed cuffs. These items, especially the fringed cuffs, definitely altered his appearance and accented his movements. Trey knew they would not hamper his body cues and weight shifts that were what Star responded to, but he knew it was best to introduce anything new and potentially scary before trying to mount a spooked horse. Star stretched his muzzle toward the new items and sniffed at each one, then realizing there was nothing to be alarmed about, let loose with a snot blowing snort and turned away from his trainer and friend. Wiping his face with his palms and drying them on

Star's coat, Trey said, "I guess that was your snort of approval, but ya didn't have to get it all over me, ya big lummox."

The next two hours were spent with the usual routine of review of each of the exercises and running through the complete program a couple of times. Their familiarity and confidence increased with each repetition and both horse and rider were very comfortable with the routine. The first to arrive for the big rehearsal was the trio of artisans accompanied by Skye. She assisted the three grandmothers to a seat in the bleachers, spreading blankets on the rough wood seats for a little added comfort. As they were being seated, Trey saw his mom's car enter the arena grounds followed closely by the pastor's jeep. With his mom's help, his dad negotiated the steps and short walk into the bleachers with his crutches, then dropped to his seat and placed his crutches down beside him. He was winded but he expressed how good it was to be out of the house. When his impromptu crowd of spectators was seated and he got the high sign from Skye, Trey walked Star to the front of the crowd for his parents and pastor to see his costume and to give a brief explanation of his program.

Positioning himself by the entry gate, he pictured the arena as if the judges were seated with the crowd, mentally walked through the patterns, then giving a slight leg squeeze, gigged Star to a trot along the fence toward the announcers booth. With a sharp turn to face the bleachers, he clicked Star to a full canter toward the bleachers and as they approached, dropped to a sliding stop just short of the railing. With a quick back stepping movement, they began the rest of the routine of spins, stops, rollbacks and figure eight at a canter with lead changes. The final move was another sliding stop in front of the bleachers and backing up to a stop and rest.

Both horse and rider were breathing heavily and all present were certain that Star had the bigger smile of the two. Everyone clapped and shouted cheers as their approval of the performance.

Walking Star to the fence to chat with his friends and family, Trey especially watched his father to see what his response was, and Trey did not know what to expect. It seemed in the past, if his father ever offered any praise, it always came with a qualifier that usually began with a ". . . but" and followed by some comment for improvement or criticism of whatever was done and could have been better. Now, Trey gratefully listened as the grandmothers and Pastor Adams offered their words of praise and wonder. With an occasional heaving chest grabbing for more air, he replied repeatedly with "Thanks, thanks a bunch," and leaning down to pat Star on the side of the neck would add, "It's all because of this guy."

As he lifted his head, he gave a sidelong glance to his father and watched as he struggled to stand with his crutches. With the hobbling gait, his father came closer to the fence and looking at his son, he said, "I'm impressed. That was something special." Trey was relieved to hear his father's comment of approval and started to answer but was stopped as his father continued, "But why no saddle or bridle or at least a bosal? It seems you'd have better control with something in your hands."

Trey looked at his father, dropped his eyes to his horse's withers and reached down to pat Star on the neck as a reward for the hard work. Then he swung his leg around over the rump of the horse and dropped to the ground. As he started to approach the fence, Skye called out, "What'd you do, wet your pants?"

Trey looked down at his leggings, lifted the breech cloth and saw the inside of both his legs and his crotch were wet through the leather leaving a dark color with the dampness. He quickly realized the hard work out caused Star to work up his usual sweat and his new buckskins absorbed most of it. The muted laughter of the crowd caused him to look up embarrassed to be rescued from the moment by his Grandmother saying, "Ah, that's just a little horse sweat. We can fix that with a good dose of saddle soap. Hurry up and take them things off so we can git 'em dried out and put on a good coat of saddle soap."

Trey turned to Star and said, "All right, Mr. Sweaty, come on," as he jogged to the holding pen to his saddle bags and other clothes. When he returned to the bleachers to hand over his leggings, his dad was making his way down the steps beside his mother and heading to their car. Trey called out to them, "I'll be home in a little bit!" A wave over his shoulder from his dad signaled his approval and he disappeared around the bleachers. Turning to his Grandmother, he passed the leggings through the rails to her outstretched hands. She grasped his hand to get his attention and said, "I know that's not what you wanted ta hear from your dad, but be patient with him. He didn't get much encouragement from his daddy and he don't know how ta give it. But he'll learn. You just keep doin' whatchur doin' cuz your Grandmother is real proud of you."

Chapter 25: Pioneer Days

WITH THE NEAPOLITAN POPULATION of the Lander valley, different activities and events took priority at special times of the social calendar. This week involved everyone with the many programs for all ages, cultures and interests. The climax of the week came on Saturday night with the world's oldest paid rodeo. The organizers of the Pioneer Days did all they could to have something to include every population strata of the community. The blend of cultures and interests began with a craft show in the park, followed by a buffalo barbecue and a 5k run into the nearby mountains. That blend again showed itself during the Saturday activities that started off with a street pancake breakfast, leading into a citywide parade, then to the fair grounds for the horse show and reining competition and would meet its grand finale with the night's rodeo.

Skye and her mom along with Trey and his mom and dad arranged their lawn chairs near the curb in front of the insurance office on Main Street to ready themselves to enjoy the big parade. They would have time to enjoy the parade, usually lasting up to two hours, and still return home and meet Pastor Adams and load Star to go to the fairgrounds for the competition. Now was the time to relax, focus on something other than Star and the big event, and enjoy the company of family and friends. Skye volunteered for Trey and her to go down the street to a vendor and get everyone something to drink and the parents happily dug into pockets and purses to retrieve the necessary money. Walking together and making their way through the gathering crowd, Skye tried in vain to carry on a conversation with Trey. Too many people in too small a place made the crowded sidewalk a poor place to talk privately. The vendor was actually a small ice cream and coffee shop on a popular corner of the busy street, and was enjoying a brisk business with several people waiting in line. Finally, Skye and Trey stood together and Skye asked, "So, are you getting nervous?" as she referred to the Free Style competition coming up in just a few hours.

"I don't know, mebbe a little. I just hope Star doesn't get as nervous as me," replied Trey as he turned his head away to browse the nearby crowd. Whenever he looked straight at Skye, he couldn't keep his mind on what he was supposed to be doing or saying and would usually end up fidgeting or tongue tied. He was comfortable with her and when they were by themselves, he didn't have those problems, but whenever anyone was around, whether he knew them or not, he reverted back to his shell of self-protection.

"Ah, you're gonna do great. I don't have any doubt about it. You and that horse are so good together, and when you're out there in that arena it's like there's nobody else in the world but the two of you," she said encouragingly. She often thought about Trey and the way he froze up around crowds and especially strangers. There was so much history with him and times of embarrassment in situations where the attention was on him and he felt unable or hindered by what others perceived as a disability. She had prayed for him and had her prayer partners in the youth group at church committed to pray for him and today's big event. It wasn't that she thought she should pray for him to win, but to just do his best and not have it turn into a traumatic or embarrassing time. She had learned much about Dyslexia since the Pastor started working with Trey this summer and knew that it was not a disability but just a different way that his brain worked. Trey had worked hard all summer and learned how to adapt his "free-thinking" to his everyday activities and especially to the training of Star. What she had been a witness to was nothing short of amazing to her, and she was proud of her friend and the victory she saw in him and the work with Star. At times, she dared to dream about what could happen with the event today and perhaps others bigger than today, but she did not share them with anyone, even Trey.

The majorettes and flag-bearers from the local high school band led the parade with considerable fanfare by trumpets and trombones sounding out with patriotic numbers. Convertibles with dignitaries, local government officials, and politicians were close behind. A visiting Shriner's club with miniature cars buzzing around preceded the local mounted sheriff's possee. About 20 bearded and buckskin attired mountain men carried flintlock rifles and led pack mules with beaver plews to represent the Mountain Man Rendevous. They were followed by several members of the Shoshone Rodeo Club mounted and attired appropriately to promote their upcoming all Indian rodeo. Interspersed throughout were crepe paper stuffed floats representing various businesses and organizations like the Kiwanis club and Rotary and a couple of floats by local churches. It was a pretty typical small town parade that was noted as much for the social activity as for the participants of the parade.

When the last fire truck passed by most interpreted that as a signal the parade was over and everyone started packing up their paraphernalia and lawn chairs to try to beat the traffic. Small town folks interpreted a five minute delay to be a major traffic jam and most would take alternate routes on the back roads. Trey followed his mom and dad to the car carrying the lawn chairs and walking beside Skye. Before moving away to join her mom, Skye said, "I'll be over as soon as we get home.

I want to take out the braids in Star's mane and comb it out. O.K.?

"Sure. I'll see you there. By the way, what time did Pastor say he was coming by?" Trey asked.

"Lunch time or shortly after. That'll give you plenty of time."

She squeezed his hand and waved with the other as she followed her mom to their car. The trip from downtown to their home was about twenty minutes and was traveled in silence. With his dad in the passenger seat, Trey watched from the rear seat and noticed his dad reaching down to move his cast to a more comfortable position, the grimace on his face revealing his discomfort. "Do you still have a lotta pain, Dad?" asked Trey.

"Just every now and then. Not too bad, right now the itching that I can't reach bothers me more. It's a big time aggravation," Stoney stated and he grunted and squirmed to a new position.

"Are you gonna be able to make it to the show today?"

"Son, I'll do everything I can to see you do your thing today. Ain't nuthin' keepin' me away from that!"

Trey was surprised to hear the adamant speech from his father. Stoney had never put much of a priority on attending anything that Trey was involved with before, but Trey was happy to hear his dad state with such certainty that he was going to see him today. For Trey, this wasn't the culmination of everything, but just another step. What he envisioned, what he dreamed, was much more than just this one event. He didn't know if he would ever have an opportunity to see his vision become reality, but he and Star had already done more than he would have imagined just a few months ago. After the last run-in with Mark Blackman and his buddies at the end of school, he hadn't thought much about it. But it seemed like there was so much that happened, the suspension, the conference with Mr. Whitson and his "disability" talk, then finding Star and meeting the pastor, all those things had made him different. He had grown in so many ways and now saw everything and everyone through what, different eyes? Maybe it was just that he was no longer focused on other people or other events, but had focused on what his world had become and what he was learning. Yeah, things were different and now with Star and the competition he was going to show everyone just how different.

Arriving at the house, Trey grabbed the folding chairs from the trunk and took them to the back of the house, then returned to the car to help his dad with his crutches to climb the front steps and into the house. His dad made it to the couch and informed everyone he was going to "rest his eyes" a bit as he stretched out to a more comfortable position. Trey went through the kitchen and out the back door to ready Star for the trip into town. It was just a few minutes later he heard the pastor's truck and trailer bouncing up the rutted road to their house. Picking the lead rope from the top rail, he reached over to hook it to the metal ring at the bottom of Star's halter, then opened the gate and led Star to the front of the house.

Skye arrived just before they loaded Star into the trailer and she decided to throw her grooming kit into the rear seat of the truck in anticipation of finishing her grooming after they finished the trip. After about a 30 minute drive, they arrived at the Rodeo grounds on the South side of Lander. Several rigs were parked on the West end of the property and several had horses tethered to the trailers with many under the shade of extended awnings from the trailers. The pastor pulled his trailer in line with the others and all three stepped out to start unloading both horses and gear. Just for comfort sake and to add a little familiarity, they brought Pepper to give Star some company. Trey tethered both horses on the shady side of the trailer and started saddling Pepper while Skye carried her grooming kit and sat it near Star to begin her work. Small talk about the different rigs and horses and questions about schedules kept their minds occupied as they readied for the big event.

"Trey, you're entered in the Non-Pro class since this is your first event. The other class is the Open class and that's where you'll find all those that do this on a regular basis. Some of them have been doin' it for years and have literally spent a fortune on horses and tack. But, you don't have to be concerned about them, I think there's only four or five in the Non-Pro class," surmised the pastor.

"We're judged the same way, though, aren't we? I mean on the same point system and all?" inquired Trey.

"Yeah. And the winner will actually qualify for the championship at the State Fair."

"Do they have the same classes at the Fair?" asked Trey.

"Yeah, but the difference is, once you qualify you have the choice to enter either in the Non-Pro or the Open class. Course, the prize money is more in the Open," observed Pastor Adams.

"Well, I ain't worried 'bout that. Today is all I'm concerned with right now," mumbled Trey in return.

Skye had listened to the conversation and now allowed her mind to wander back to what Trey had shared with her about his vision and the Eagle Dance comparison. *Wouldn't that be something if he could go to the State Championships and go all out with his Eagle vision.* With her mind's eye she could see Trey's vision come to life while she mindlessly combed out the braids from Star's mane. "Hey, you're gonna pull all the hair out if you keep that up!" warned Trey as he noticed Skye's enthusiastic combing. Startled, she looked at him, then back at Star and said, "I'm sorry, I was just thinkin' " she said, then busied herself with the task at hand.

"As soon as the horse show part is over and before the regular reining begins, there will be about a half hour that the arena if free. That would be a good time to lead Star around the arena with Pepper and let him kind of get familiar with everything," the pastor informed Trey. With a nodded response, Trey finished cinching down the saddle on Pepper. "We'll be able to watch some of the reining before the Free Style begins. The Open class goes first, and I think there are seven or eight of those, then your class follows. We can even watch some of the Open class if you want."

"Sure, sounds good to me. Don't you want to see them Skye?" asked Trey. He knew she planned to help him with the costume and other preparations for his part, but he also wanted her to see the rest of the class so he could get her feed-back on their performance as well. Skye knew what he was thinking and she was determined to help in any way she could.

The next few hours seemed to fly by and the Free Style competition was being announced over the loudspeakers. They stayed by the fence for the first three contestants and Trey was entranced at the performances of the three women that were the first performers. Each was attired in similar outfits with long flowing capes and gowns that emphasized the movements of the horses. The accompaniment music was usually some classical type with string instruments and dramatic sounds. After each performance, the judges scores were tallied and announced before announcing the next contestant. The announcer then said, "And the next contestant is a familiar face and a local boy, Mark Blackman aboard Peppy's Irish Doll." Trey looked at Skye, and shaking his head, he turned to go to the trailer to prepare for his event. Skye followed him and spoke to his back, "Trey, don't even think about him. 'sides, he's in the other class and you're not competing with him."

"I know. I'm not doin' this for him anyway. It has nothing to do with him," he said as he opened the side door to the dressing room on the trailer. Trey soon exited the trailer and handed Skye the hairpiece, headband, and cuffs for her assistance in completing his costume. When he was attired, the two led Star to the West end of the arena to the entry gate where other contestants awaited. As they stood waiting, Mark Blackman exited the arena after his performance and passing Trey, he looked down and with a snide expression said, "What are you doin' here?"

Trey chose to look toward the arena as if he had not heard the remark, but Skye was not to be ignored as she retorted,

"He's here to show you how it's supposed to be done. Don't you wanna watch and learn something'?"

Mark, attired in his Roy Rogers lookalike outfit, looked down at Trey and simply said, "Hah! That'll be the day!" then gigged his horse toward his trailer.

Trey looked back at Skye and shook his head as a grin tugged at the corners of his mouth. All too soon, the last contestant before Trey was entering the arena and Trey needed to mount up. As Skye held the lead rope, Trey did his usual little hop and belly mount and swinging his leg over Star's rump, he settled in to the familiar seat aboard Star. As the other contestant exited the arena, he waited for the announcer as he said, "And now, another local boy with his first time entry, Trey Standingelk." With a nod to Skye, she slipped the halter over Star's head and stepped aside. The usual leg squeeze started Star to the arena and the familiar routine.

The center of the South side of the arena was the bucking chutes with the announcer's booth above. The judges were seated on tall stools in front of the chutes and spaced out about thirty feet. The bleachers were on both sides of the chutes giving the spectators a good view of the entire arena. The music chosen by Trey was a combination of Indian flute and pan pipes and had a definite Native American tune, but the music was a perfect accompaniment for his program. Their entry was impressive with the full canter ending in the sliding stop between the judges, then a quick back up before beginning the figure eight with the lead changes. After the large circles were completed flawlessly, the two spins in the middle of the arena brought oohs and awwws from the crowd, then the duo accelerated to the East end and did a dramatic sliding stop followed by a roll back and another full speed gallop to the West end for the final sliding stop with a back-up and rest. Leaning over the neck of Star, Trey spoke to his horse as he petted his neck and said, "Good job, boy. We did it!" As they exited the arena, the announcer said, "Folks, I don't know if you noticed, but that last contestant did the entire routine without any tack whatsoever on that horse! No, it's not unusual for a contestant to do their program without a bridle, but that boy didn't even have a saddle! Now, are you ready for the final results? The score on the last contestant, Trey Standingelk, put him in first place! How's that for a home town boy?" Trey had already exited the arena and wasn't even listening to the announcer. While he rode Star toward the trailer, Skye walked alongside and reached up to hold Trey's hand. "You were great! You and Star did everything just perfect! I am so proud of you!" she exclaimed.

At the trailer, he dropped off the back of Star and started toward the dressing room to change his clothes when he heard the pastor calling, "Hey you two! What're ya doin'? You gotta go back out there."

Trey and Skye looked at him with brows furrowed in question, "Huh?"

"Didn't you hear? You won! Ya gotta go get your prize buckle, now git out there!" he stated with a big smile stretched across his usual somber face.

Star Dancer

Chapter 26: Decision

STATE CHAMPIONSHIPS. That's going to take some thought and if it's to be done, a lot of preparation, thought Trey. He was riding in the passenger seat of Pastor Adam's truck as they were heading back to Trey's house with Star in the trailer following along behind. *Maybe this is what it was all leading up to, this could be the vision I had.* The Pastor had been watching Trey knowing his mind was working overtime on everything that had happened today. He knew the boy was a bit overwhelmed with so many emotions coming in on the evening tide, it was a lot for a 15 year old to comprehend and to consider. He was proud of Trey and what he had accomplished with Star but more so for the way he had risen to the challenge of mastering the extra hurdle life had thrown his way, Dyslexia. "Trey, what you need to do now is just take some time to let it all sink in before you make any decision about what you're going to do next. I'd like to see you at church in the morning, if you can, 'cause there's a lot of folks there that have been prayin' for you and they'd like to hear how you did today. But, you only need to do what's comfortable for you, O.K.? Just think about it, and let me know," stated the pastor. He pulled the truck to a stop and exited the truck to help Trey as he unloaded the horses. "I think he deserves an extra helping of grain for the job he did today," said the pastor as he stroked Star's neck while Trey led him around to the corral. "He's quite a horse, of course, you already know that."

Trey looked at the pastor with a wide smile and a special sparkle in his eyes as he opened the gate to turn Star into the corral with Pepper. Both horses walked to the feeder looking for their evening rations and turned to look back at Trey as if asking him to serve up their supper. He forked them a couple of flakes of hay and put a portion of grain in the trough for both horses. Turning to the pastor waiting at the gate, he said, "I'll be at church in the morning, but I don't think I'm ready to talk to the people. Can you just tell 'em what happened and thank 'em for the prayers?"

"No problem, Trey. I understand."

Trey walked with the pastor back to his truck and said, "Pastor, I really appreciate all you've done. This wouldn't have been possible without your help, I know that, and I'm thankful." The pastor knew Trey was talking about more than just today's event, and he understood how hard it was for him to express himself to the full extent of what he was feeling. The pastor remembered when he had those same experiences and the challenge he faced to overcome what so many still perceived as a disability. His greatest fear had been talking or reading in front of people, and now he did it every week. He had always been faithful to give God the glory and the praise for the victory, but he also knew Trey was not at that point in his spiritual life. He also knew it was not something that could be pushed on him, either the spiritual part or the talking part like sharing in front of the crowd.

"Well, I'll see you in the mornin' then," said the pastor as he turned his truck to return to Lander and waved at Trey as he pulled away. Skye had stayed in town with her mom to go to the rodeo that night and Trey's folks were still in town, leaving Trey alone with his thoughts about everything that happened today. He hadn't really thought about winning the competition,

170

his reason for participating was just the culmination of all the training and work with Star. The event was like the final finish coat on a piece of woodwork, just something to savor and appreciate. He sat the box with the trophy belt buckle down on the coffee table and removed the top to see the multi colored carved metal belt buckle before him. A copper banner across the top declared "Lander Pioneer Days" while another banner across the bottom said, "Non-Pro Free Style Reining Champion." In the center was a bronze colored figure of a man mounted on a horse maneuvering a bend causing the figure to lean to the right. It was a prize to be proud of like the many others worn by winners of other rodeo type events, but Trey wasn't certain if he would wear it or just put it on display on a shelf in his room. *Oh well, that's a decision for another day.*

He went into the kitchen, opened the refrigerator door and stood looking at the shelves and the food they held. Without moving for a couple of minutes, and with nothing jumping into his arms and saying "eat me!", he reached for a can of cola and shut the door. He returned to the couch and pushed one of his dad's pillows under his arm, searched for the TV remote, found it and turned on the TV. He looked out the window as his eyes covered over with a glassy stare and his mind wandered to his vision of the Eagle Dance and how he had imagined combining the dance and the Free Style performance into one special program. What he now saw was exactly what he had initially envisioned when he first saw the free style competition in Cody. With the outstretched wings of his imagined costume, he and star soared through the program in his vision and with the moves to be made, he saw himself honoring the ancient beliefs and dance of his ancestors. He decision was made for him, he was going to the State championships.

In the early part of the service, Pastor Adams had shared the news about Trey's winning performance and that he had qualified for the State Championship. While he was talking he looked at Trey several times and when he mentioned the championship, he saw Trey nodding his head up and down to signal his decision. "So, Trey, does that mean that you've made your decision?" again with the head nod, "So, you're going to the State Championship?" With a broad smile, Trey again nodded his head and mouthed a yes. "Well, folks, looks like our prayin' ain't over. We've got about three weeks ahead of us to keep him in prayer." Several people turned to look at Trey and gave him a thumbs up sign to show their approval. Skye reached for his hand and squeezed it to show her happiness with his decision, and she smiled as he turned to face her. "'You're gonna have to help me, ya know," he whispered to her.

"You don't think I'd let ya even try it without me, do ya?" she replied.

Trey had packed his costume in his warbag, with the exception of his roach headpiece, for Skye to take to his Grandmother's to meet with the ladies that had made the costume. As she sat at the kitchen table, she used her sketch pad to illustrate to the ladies all the changes and additions that were needed. After first hearing Trey describe his vision for the program, she had been visualizing what the costume should look like and the extent of the decorations. As he explained to her, his vision was to replicate the Eagle Dance and costume as used by those participating in the special tribal Eagle Dance. Historically, the dance was symbolic of the eagle carrying the prayers of the people to the creator. The performance of the dance symbolized the life and actions of the eagle from birth through the times of hunting to the soaring high to the creator. Some felt the eagle was also a symbol of bravery and honor and the use of the eagle's feathers in their adornment reflected the greatness of the warrior. Skye's part was to make the costume not only fulfill the vision, but to be usable horseback. Since hearing his decision and asking for her help, she could think of nothing else and the many possibilities for his attire swirled through her mind constantly. Now it was time to put it on paper and let the group of grandmotherly artisans know what was being asked of them.

As she completed her sketches and turned the sketch pad for their viewing, she watched as they looked, reached to touch, and commented. They had never had the opportunity to do this type of costume and the possibilities and challenges were evident in their expressions and comments. Yet each one literally raised her head, rolled her shoulders back, and in her own unique way said, "Well, let's get to work!" With a deep breath and a long sigh, Skye showed her relief and joy at what lie before them. As usual, Grandmother Standingelk took charge and said, "All right, let's make a list of what we're gonna need, especially how many feathers!" Turning to Skye, she said, "And as for you, young lady, you're gonna need to get that boy here for some more measurin' before we can go too far."

With a broad smile she said, "Yes, Grandmother. I'm gonna see him today and I'll get him to come probably this afternoon. O.K.?" After Grandmother answered with a nod of her head and a bit of a grunt, Skye rose from her chair and headed for the front door. She had agreed to meet Trey at his home so they could talk about the program and what he wanted to change. The State Championships were just three weeks away, but that did not allow a full three weeks of training. She was hopeful he didn't have major changes he wanted to try, but she knew his vision was more than the performance at Pioneer Days. As she thought about it, she realized her excitement level was rising and she wasn't sure she would be able to keep it in check. Of course, there really wasn't any alternative. It was exciting to be a part of it all. As she pondered it all, she thought, *The State Championships, who woulda thought? I always envied the connection he seemed to have with horses, but I never dreamed about anything like this. Oh, I hope he is able to live his dream!*

Star Dancer

Chapter 27: Revision

NOW AT TREY'S KITCHEN table, Skye asked, "So, what changes are you gonna make?"

"Well, there's a couple of simple moves that I wanna add for the entrance, and one at the end. But I'm gonna need the pastor's help with some of it. Ya think he'd mind givin' me a hand?" asked Trey. He was pretty certain that Pastor Adams would be happy to help, but Skye was closer to him and had known him longer, so Trey was hoping Skye would intercede for him with the pastor.

"I'm sure he would. Just what did you have in mind?"

"Well, I'd kinda like ta keep it a surprise, if ya don't mind. It's sumpin' special for you." He smiled at her and ducked his head to hide his blushing as he felt the heat rise to his face.

"So, what did you need me here for, then?

"Well, I wanna go over the rest of it with you. You're the only one that can see it like I can and I just need to run it by you and see whatcha think," he implored. "So, could you call the pastor for me?"

"You big chicken. All right, I'll do it. But you owe me!" she replied.

It only took a few minutes for Trey to fill her in on the changes as she drew the program pattern on the sketchpad. The main difference was on the entry with a couple of new steps to add a little flair to the entry, then at the ending of the program he would do a lap around the arena and finish with a sliding stop in front of the grandstands and the crowd. Skye expressed her approval and excitement about the program and admonished him to get busy with the training and the practice. She agreed to set up the time for the pastor to join him and would try for this afternoon. Saying their goodbyes, Skye left to rejoin the crafty group of grandmothers and Trey went to ready Star and Pepper for the day's work at the arena.

Much of what goes on between a horse and rider has to do with body cues. In reining especially the body cues are even more important as the contestants are scored on the amount of evident control due to the use of tack versus body cues. The saddle used by a reiner is a special light weight with thinner skirt, fenders, and even the seat. This is to provide better contact between the rider and the horse exemplifying the body cues for better control. Most reiners use leg cues, the pressure from either leg to cue the horse to move away from the pressure, and often use the cues of weight shifts to precede a sliding stop or other maneuvers. In comparison to the typical reiner, the communication between Star and Trey was amplified by the lack of any tack. The close contact between the two was not hindered by saddle, blanket or any other tack. Star was able to feel the slightest move, touch, or weight shift on the part of his rider and had grown accustomed to the requested move on the part of Trey. Now it was time to add to the repertoire as Trey began to introduce Star to the added maneuvers for the new extended program for the State Championships.

The first two hours went by quickly and prompted Trey to trot Star to the holding pen and the awaiting trough of water. Pepper greeted the two with a low whinney as he trotted to the gate and waited for Trey to open the barrier between them.

With a nod of his head, Star made his way to the water trough as Trey slipped off and headed to his shoulder bag and his water bottle. Both horse and rider showed the evidence of a work-out with the sweat outline of Trey's legs on the back and ribs of Star and Star's sweat on the inside of Trey's trouser legs. Tilting his head back to chug the water, he noticed the dust cloud following the pastor's jeep as he wheeled into the arena parking lot. With a wave at the pastor, Trey led Star back to the arena and to the entry gate where the pastor now waited.

"I see you're already hard at work. How's it going?" asked Pastor Adams as he stepped through the gate to join the pair.

"Good. You're just in time. We just finished the work on the first steps, and now will be a great time to get started on the next thing," replied the young trainer.

"And just what is this 'next thing' that you need my help with?"

"Well, you know how when you're doin' your preachin' thing, and at the end when you pray, you have your horse kinda take a bow? That's what I want to do at the end of the program," stated Trey with a big smile showing his ever present enthusiasm.

"Whoa. You're not askin' much. You've got what, less than three weeks before State and you wanna add that move? "

"Yeah, do ya really think I'm askin' too much?" he questioned with an expression that betrayed his concern.

The pastor looked at his protégé and thought for a few moments, dropping his gaze to the ground as he pondered the proposal. This horse and boy had already defied all odds and accomplished more than most professional trainers would have even attempted. The diligence and commitment were not the question, but the time remaining was a big question. It was not just mastering this extraordinary move, but the additional moves he had already introduced as well as the necessary continued practice on the core program. The last thing he wanted to do was to disappoint Trey by telling him it would be too difficult for him, that would be taken as a lack of confidence. Trey had already shown his ability to rise to the challenge, no matter the task and whatever was required, he delivered. Now was no time to take the wind out of his sails. "O.K., then, I guess we better get to work."

The rest of the afternoon was spent working on this difficult maneuver. With the pastor on the ground giving directions and stepping in to manhandle Star when needed, and Trey on top of Star working on the necessary leg cues, finally by the end of the day, a successful move. Trotting up to a stop, extending his left foreleg at Trey's cue with his toe behind Star's elbow, stepping back with his hind legs and tucking his right foreleg under his chest and dropping his muzzle down to bring his chin against his chest Star performed a perfect bow and held it until Trey clucked him upright.

"Wow, if anyone would have told me this was possible this quickly, I would've told them they were crazy!" stated the pastor. "Course, this is just the first one. You're gonna have to work on this every day until he gets it so smooth it'll look like a dance step."

"Thanks Pastor. You know we'll be workin' on this and everything else every day," stated Trey showing his resolve. The trio now walked to the holding pen to finish the day of practice with a long drink of water. Trey handed the pastor a fresh bottle of water and proceeded to finish off the one he started on earlier.

"By the way, Trey, I've been wantin' to talk to you. You've heard me preach a few messages on Sundays and we've talked about the scriptures with you reading work, but I wouldn't be doin' my job if I didn't ask you," stated the pastor.

"Ask me what, pastor?"

"Well, I know you have held to the beliefs of your people and that's a good thing. But sometimes that doesn't go far enough. You know I've said before, that your relationship with God is a personal thing, but it's more than just believing in the Creator as you call Him, it's accepting what He has to say in His word. That is, what the Bible says about Jesus. There should be a time in your life that you accept what Jesus did on the cross and know that it was for you. When you ask God to forgive you of your sins and accept the free gift of salvation that Jesus offers to each of us, that's how you begin that personal relationship with Christ. Do you understand that Trey?" he asked as he watched Trey turn to look at the distant clouds in the broad blue sky overhead.

"Yes, I understand that. I've been thinkin' about it a lot. That's part of what prompted this program. My people see Eagle as a symbol of courage and honor, but more than that, the flight of the eagle is heavenward, and as he soars upward, he carries our prayers to the Creator. I've kinda thought about it like that. When I do this, I honor my people, give homage to my ancestors and the ancients, but I also see a new beginning as the eagle carries my prayers to the Creator. That prayer you speak of to ask God for forgiveness and to accept His gift, I see it being carried upon the wings of the eagle that I will represent. Do you understand?"

The pastor was silent and stirred. Here this young man in his simple belief and understanding was showing more pure faith than he had seen in anyone in a long time. He knew it wasn't the words of the prayer, or the years of practice, or the depth of knowledge of scriptures, but the pure and simple belief of the heart. He placed his hand on Trey's shoulder and simply said, "Yes, I understand. Thanks for sharing that with me."

Grandmother was a kind and loving woman, but she also had a stern and authoritative side that came out now as she confronted her grandson. "So help me, boy, if you mess this one up, we ain't got time ta do another. You hear me?" she questioned as she tried hard to be firm with the grandson that knew nothing but love from her.

"Yes, Grandmother, I understand. This will work great."

"Well, when Skye told us you needed a set of 'practice wings' I thought you were just addin' more work for us, but after I got to thinkin' about it, I knew she was right. Now this

179

set ain't as fancy and don't have as many feathers, but it should do for you to practice with. Just how are you gonna practice with 'em, anyway?"

"It's mainly to get Star used to 'em, Grandmother. Because they'll be such a part of the performance, I don't want him gittin' spooked by 'em. And some of the cues I use will have to be changed a bit cuz of the wings. We just need to practice with 'em to get used to 'em."

"Well, O.K. then, and don't forget, there's just a little over a week left, and you've gotta come in for a final fittin' on the rest of this getup, so we'll have time to do any fixin' that needs to be done before you go," she warned him.

Turning to the other ladies he asked, "You're all gonna be there aren't you?" The nodding heads and mumbled answers were what he wanted to hear, he was counting on friends and family to take away the fear of the bigger crowd that would be at the arena. He asked the same question of just about everyone he spoke to during the final days of practice. He was pleased to hear so many give their encouragement and affirm their plan of being present. Skye walked him to the door and outside as she asked him, "Is the practice going O.K.? I'm sorry I haven't been there more, but these ladies have been keepin' me pretty busy. You don't mind do you?"

"No, to be honest with you, we've been so focused, I usually forget to stop for lunch until Star reminds me with a nip or two. But it's been going pretty good. I think we'll have it down in time."

"Trey, I can't tell you how proud I am of you. What you've done in these few months have been amazing and I'm so glad you are going to realize the vision you told me about. Not everyone gets to see their dream become real."

"If it wasn't for you and all you've done, it wouldn't be. It all started cuz you wanted to see those petroglyphs, remember?" he reminded her. It now seemed so long ago when they took that ride to the cliffs and saw the wild horse herd and the first sighting of Star.

"I remember. How can I forget? That day seems to have changed both our lives. Are you happy?" she asked, as she looked up at him. His long black hair shielded his face, but he turned to look directly at her and said, "You make me happy."

Star Dancer

Chapter 28: State Fair

LONG DAYS, SHORT WEEKS, and now Trey was looking out the front window of his home waiting to see the pastor's truck and trailer coming up their road. Everything still seemed like a dream, something that he never considered, not in his wildest imagination would he have ever contemplated the possibility that he would be going to the state fair and the championship competition for Free Style reining. Last year at this time, he didn't even know what Free Style reining was and certainly never thought he would be a part of anything like this type of an event. Competition of any type was not in Trey's mindset. He would rather be a loner and get on his horse and go to the mountains away from everything and everyone. That had been his escape since he was old enough to be trusted by his mom to be on his own. Different from the city kids, Trey took to the wilderness and often sought the refuge to be found in solitude in the mountains. The only one he shared that time with was his lifelong friend, Skye. Her friendship and companionship made him feel complete and confident. And now, she had been a very special part of this chapter of his life, his life that now was changing beyond anything he ever dreamed.

Dragging a bit of a dust cloud behind him, the pastor's truck and trailer bounced their way up the rutted dirt road. At this time of year their long road and driveway took on the corduroy effect with more bumps and ruts than an old-fashioned washboard. Even through the dust cloud, the pastor's wide smile was evident. As the truck slowed to a stop, Trey turned to go to the corral and collect the two horses. Returning with Star and Pepper in tow, Trey saw the pastor waiting with the rear doors open for an easy load of the horses.

"So, Trey, are you as excited as I am about all this?" inquired the pastor.

"Probably, but I'm not sure if it's excitement or somebody let a bunch of butterflies loose in my gut. Course, maybe it's just that I'm a little scared, but don't tell anybody," cautioned Trey, thinking especially of Skye as he watched her climb out of the back seat of the truck. They both knew Skye already understood the emotions that showed on Trey's face, even though he worked hard to maintain a stoic appearance as expected of a Native male. Emotions were supposed to be kept in check and never revealed by a man but that was easier said than done.

The almost two hundred mile trip was made without incident, the only stop being in Casper for some fast food and to refuel. Arriving in Douglas at the Fair Grounds, they followed the signs to locate the horse stalls in the livestock shed. They parked in the designated area and unloaded the horses to take them inside and get them settled in their new accommodations. It was the day before the scheduled big event and they would have ample time for the last minute preparations and familiarizations. The second trip to the trailer brought the necessary tack, grooming gear, and war bag with costume and other necessities. While Skye carried most of the gear, Trey and Pastor Adams carried in a couple bales of hay and a bucket of grain. Settled in by mid-afternoon, Pastor suggested they take the remaining daylight and look over the various displays and programs of the State Fair.

Starting with the other livestock buildings, they toured the many stalls and booths showing the livestock and livestock support that qualified for the State Fair through county fairs and 4-H programs. The many different breeds of cattle, horses, and smaller animals were interesting to Trey as most of his life had been spent with animals of one kind or another. Skye showed special interest in the craft type displays with sewing, quilting, and home-making entries. None of the three were interested in the commercial and political displays housed in other buildings and chose instead to partake of the different food vendors along the park walkway. As dusk settled in and the many lights came on, the noise level picked up with the most noise coming from the carnival and its many dizzying rides. Preferring instead to return to the horse stalls, Trey suggested to Skye and the Pastor to continue their tour. Both declined and joined Trey on his return. It was not unusual for owners and riders to spend the night in the stalls with their animals and with sleeping bags rolled out, Skye chose to stay in the stall with Pepper while Star's companion was Trey. The Pastor had accommodations in his horse trailer that beckoned him and he was happy to have the convenience of a real bed. Before turning in for the night, Skye busily braided Star's mane and tail in anticipation of the additional grooming set for the morning. While she braided, Trey smoothed Star's coat with the brush that had become Star's favorite. Not to be neglected, Pepper peered through the dividing bars from his adjoining stall and with a deep rumble from his throat, he let his opinion be known.

"All right, all right, I'll brush you next. Be patient boy, I'm not neglecting you," reassured Trey. Pepper would earn his keep tomorrow as he accompanied Star into the arena in the morning during the free time to acquaint Star with the arena and the other horses. This time, Skye would ride Pepper while Trey rode Star to help him become familiar and comfortable with the entire facility.

"Has he always been that jealous?" asked Skye, looking at Pepper while she continued her braiding.

"Ah, he's not jealous. He just doesn't like being neglected. With both of us over here, and him by himself over there, maybe he's just lonely," replied Trey, "Guys get that way, ya know."

"Listen to you. What have you got to be lonely about?"

"Nothin' now," he replied as he grinned at Skye. "By the way, thanks."

"For what?"

"For everything. You know, the costume, the program layout, grooming Star. Mostly, for stickin' with me thru all this. Thanks." He dropped his head giving a closer look to a perceived tuft of hair that needed his attention. Skye smiled at him, even though he wasn't looking at her, and knew that what he said was just a small hint of what he was really thinking. Like most guys, he didn't find it easy to express himself, and less so because of the challenges he had been facing recently. She admitted to herself that thinking about her and Trey together was something she occasionally indulged in, even to the visualizing of the two of them many years in the future as being together as husband and wife, but these thoughts were not to be shared with anyone, even Trey.

The Pastor rousted them to wakefulness by kicking on the stall doors of each of the two stalls. With plenty of straw for bedding and warm sleeping bags, the two teens had little difficulty getting a good night's sleep, but as usual, waking up was another proposition. But when the Pastor said he had breakfast burritos and orange juice, Trey didn't hesitate to be the first to respond. Rolling up his bag, he dusted himself off, having worn everything but his boots through the night, he was ready for breakfast. Skye took a little longer to ready herself, but she soon presented her wrinkled self at the makeshift breakfast table on the hay bales.

Finishing breakfast, Trey busted one of the bales and forked a couple of flakes to each of the horses. Skye cleaned the stalls with the manure fork and raked the straw to smooth the horse's beds. Although neither horse would use the straw to lay down, it made it easier to keep the stalls clean.

"The open arena time will be during the noon hour. That'll be after the halter classes for the horses and before the other reining classes take place. So, you'll need to be ready to take advantage of the time to get Star used to the arena," informed the pastor. "That will give you a few hours before your event so you will have plenty of time to get ready. Since you chose to move up to the Open class, your group will be the last on the docket for the day. If you were still in the Non-pro class, that class goes before the Open. But I think you made the right choice. The open draws a bigger crowd also."

"I didn't know you switched to Open. How come?" asked Skye, surprised.

"I really don't know. It just seemed to be the thing to do," explained Trey. To move up to the Open class put him in the same class as those that were considered professional or those that did this all the time. Many had been competing in the Open class for several years. Although it was unusual for a rookie or beginner to move up, it was allowed to give everyone a chance at what most referred to as "the big time." The Open class had more competitors and more prize money, although money was not the reason for Trey's decision. He couldn't explain it because he wasn't sure he understood it himself, but he knew it was what was necessary. What he had envisioned was the bigger crowd and the larger class, not for the competition but to be able to fulfill his dream. Trey wasn't doing this for others, prizes, or praise. It was for himself, his vision, his goal. He wasn't what others thought of him or even what he had begun to think of himself. He was more than all that, and this was something he just had to do, to find that peace within himself, the peace of the completion of a vision.

The open arena time was for the very purpose that Trey and Skye were using if for, just to get the horses familiar with new surroundings. Although most of the crowd was gone for the lunch break, there were several that remained in the grandstands, some with a packed lunch and others just to have a seat out of the sun. The noise of the other horses and riders, the remaining crowd and occasional announcements on the loudspeakers gave the horses a feel of what it would be like when their time came. With a gentle walk around the perimeter of the arena, Skye and Trey shared their thoughts about the fair and the many events. Both talked about family and friends that were expected to come, but the only sure attendees would be the families of both Skye and Trey.

"I'm pretty sure your Grandmother and her 'crafty crew' are gonna be here, too," stated Skye. The ladies had all assured her they wouldn't miss this for anything. "Also, Mary Cloud Walker's husband is a member of the Tribal Council and if she comes, he'll be with her. Wouldn't that be great to have a member of the Council here to see the program?"

"What are you tryin' ta do? Make me more nervous than I already am?" asked Trey as he looked at her with a pretended scowl. It would be an honor to have the council represented at his program but he never expected it to happen. Just family and friends was all he hoped for, just enough familiar faces to help him feel a little more comfortable, a little more confident. But he reminded himself, this was not for others, it was between him and his vision.

As the crowd started to return and fill up the seats, the announcement came over the speakers that the open arena time would conclude within five minutes. Trey and Skye turned their mounts toward the entry gate to return to the stalls. This marked the beginning of the final preparations. Skye and the pastor would help, but most of it was up to Trey. With each passing moment, the tension and expectation rose but Trey busied himself with visualizing the program to keep his thoughts in check. *Soon* was the word that seemed to be emblazoned on the stall walls and on everything else he rested his eyes on, *soon.*

Chapter 29: Championship

THE SMALL WARM-UP arena was connected to the main performance arena with a broad alley-way that provided sufficient room for those leaving the arena to pass the waiting contestants without any contact. The announcer had just given the introduction for the upcoming event, the Free Style reining Open class. The line-up was pre-determined and usually started with returning champions and the season's high point performers. Because Trey and Star were newcomers, they were slated as the last competitors, which was exactly what Trey preferred. When they competed in the Lander Pioneer Days, they were last in the line-up but finished first in the awards. Trey wasn't concerned about the awards this time, but he did want the message of his performance to be remembered, that's what his vision required.

The schedule originally had ten performers, but one had been scratched, so now only eight were to precede Trey. Skye had assisted Trey with his costume, mainly the headpiece of the double roach and the headband of the braided band with the circular design in the front. She now examined every part of the costume, noting the additional beadwork applied by Grandmother and her friends to the vest and leggings. Skye had added feathers to the leggings with one full feather about every six inches attached to the fringe at the side of the legs. Each feather had a cluster of three tassels at the end of the feather that added to the length and movement. In a similar fashion, she had attached feathers to Star's mane and tail with the many feathers adding a festive appearance to the Sorrel Stallion.

In addition to the feathers on the leggings, the ladies added a bustle or fan of feathers to be worn at the back of Trey and attached to the waist, giving a broad fan of feathers that resembled the tail of an eagle. With the added beading on the vest, the breechcloth, and the leggings, the costume now looked much more decorative and brighter in color. Another addition was the long bright blue fringe attached to the top of the armholes of the vest and hung down over the shoulders of Trey. The Pastor joined them as they waited in line, he knew Trey would need his assistance to mount Star with the added costume wings. Skye held the folded wings awaiting the time closer to Trey's mounting. She had seen how impressive this addition to his costume was and now waited with a great deal of anticipation for everyone else to see what she thought was a magnificent figure.

The Free Style event began with the returning champion taking the arena as her music filled the stadium. It was a familiar program to Trey and company as they had seen her compete in Cody, and the program was virtually unchanged. After completing and leaving the arena, she passed by the waiting contestants and casually looked at each one as she passed, until she was beside Trey and Star, then she stopped. Looking at Trey, she said, "Impressive costume. First time?"

Nodding his head he replied, "Yeah, first time."

"I don't think I've ever seen anyone using the Native Costume, I'm gonna have to watch. Good luck!"

"Thanks, I'm gonna need it," replied Trey, watching as she left the alley-way to return to the stall area.

"Luck? You don't need luck! You and Star are great and you're gonna knock 'em dead!" affirmed Skye, grinning as broad as her petite face would allow.

Three more contestants filed by as the competition continued at a regular pace. Each one either nodded or spoke to acknowledge this newcomer to the competition. Their expressions revealed a gamut of emotions from skepticism to jealousy, but none were overly friendly. The next one leaving the arena was a familiar face and stopped to speak to Trey in his usual haughty manner, "What do you think you're doin' gettin' in the Open class. You're in over your head boy!" stated Mark Blackman as he hooked his leg over his saddle horn. He was attired in his usual Roy Rogers imitation cowboy outfit with the dangling fringe.

Trey looked away and craned to see how soon he was to enter the program, ignoring the comment of Mark. But again, Skye was not to be silenced. "You better hurry up and put your horse away so you can get back out here and see how this is supposed to be done. Lesson number 2 coming up. Don't be late, now, ya hear?" The entry of another performer allowed the remaining contestants to step forward and away from the agitator, who gigged his horse to exit the alley-way.

Another contestant entered the arena, leaving just one more before Trey. Now was the time to mount up, but first he had to put on the set of wings that were specially prepared by the loving ladies of Grandmother's circle. Turning his back to Skye, he extended his arms back as she slipped on first one side, then the other. At the length of his arms was a handhold of plastic piping similar to that used as the frame for the wings. This handhold gave him the ability to move the wings at will, including folding and extending them in a movement quite similar to the movement of the eagle they represented. The pastor dropped to one knee, extending the other knee for Trey to use as a step stool to mount. As he placed his moccasined foot on the pastor's knee, the pastor reached for his belt to steady him as he mounted Star. The practice with the wings now proved its worth as Star stood his ground without so much as a twitch of a muscle. After mounting, Trey bent down with the wings on each side of Star's neck, hugged his horse and spoke to Star and asked for the best performance of their lives. Looking up he saw the last contestant leaving the arena, and knew he was next. Now at the front of the line, he was close to the entry gate and could hear the announcer and would more easily hear his accompaniment music.

"And for our last contestant, we have a first-timer to the Open class and I'm told this is a very unique performance. What will make it especially interesting is the mount for this young man is named Star Dancer and less than a year ago, this horse was part of a wild mustang herd. Ladies and Gentlemen, meet Trey Standingelk." At the last word of the announcer, the accompaniment began. The first part of the accompaniment was the far-off cry of an eagle, then the Indian flute started with its enchanting melody.

Trey and Star entered with Trey bent over Star's neck and wings down by the front legs. Star started with a high prancing step with one foreleg lifted as high as his chest and extended out in front. Then dropping that leg, brought up the other, and continued with this high step as Trey sat upright and brought the wings back, then fluttered the wings in time with the step.

As the young eaglet tests its wings for the first time in the safety of its nest . . .

Then Trey cued Star to do a half-pass to the left, as he did Star would side step at a forward angle and cross his legs with each step, keeping his head tucked to the same side as the half-pass. After six steps to the left, the maneuver was duplicated to the right. Trey changed the flutter of the wings to mimic a young bird gaining confidence and considering leaving the nest. After the half-pass maneuver, at Trey's cue, Star arched his neck and tucked his muzzle to his chest, then starting at a trot then to a full run headed straight to the fence in front of the grandstands and between the judges seated on their elevated seats, then with a stretch of his neck and dropping his hindquarters, came to a perfect sliding stop. During this part of the exercise, Trey spread his wings, flapped them in concert with Star's move and leaning far forward, sat back a spread the wings wide as Star slid to a stop.

. . . the first flight of the fledgling eaglet ends with a sudden stop upon the ground . . .

With the back-up steps accompanied by the flutter of wings, Star backed to the center of the arena, then with the inside wing dropped and the outside wing outstretched, they broke into a full canter to the figure eight and the necessary change of leads. At the center of the figure, the wing position switched to reflect the change of direction and with a good lean to the inside the movement was magnified. The music continued with the mood of the program and enhanced each move of the duo.

. . . the first flight of victory for the young eagle testing his wings . . .

Coming out of the figure eight maneuver, they accelerated in a straight line to the roping chute end of the arena, Trey now flapping his wings in a smoother movement and reflected the practiced flight of a maturing eagle, the sliding stop ended with a roll-back.

. . . the first catch of small prey as the eagle scoops his prize from the ground . . .

Now into a full run the length of the arena ending in another sliding stop and roll-back brought the team to the center of the arena. Stopping and facing the judges, they went into a full spin to the left with four complete spins, as Trey fluttered the outside wing and held the inside wing down to the side. After another stop, they duplicated this maneuver to the right.

. . . at maturity, the eagle must build a nest for his mate and family. . .

With the required moves completed, they now started in a trot in a circle, then into larger circles and faster with each one until the final circle encompassed the size of the arena. With each one, Trey seemed to rise higher and higher as he smoothly used his wings as if flying on thermal currents and rising higher in the sky. After the first sliding stop, unknown to Trey, the entire crowd seemed to pause and look. By this time, there was no movement on the part of the grandstands full of people and others watching from the surrounding fence. Some would say they couldn't even hear anyone breathing. This performance was so different, so perfect, and so impressive, no one wanted to miss a single move. Slowly the crowd rose to their feet and seemed to lean forward to get closer to what they now witnessed. There were no flashes from cameras, no cries from food vendors, no whining from children. Everyone was focused on the flight of the eagle.

. . . climbing ever higher, the eagle delivers the prayers to the Creator . . .

Completing the final circle, they turned to again approach the fence in front of the grandstand and the point between the judges. Slowing to a trot, then a walk, Star again arched his neck, tucked his muzzle to his chest and in four high prancing steps came to a stop. At the cue, he stretched his left foreleg, tucked his right foreleg to his chest, and tucked his muzzle down to the ground and executed a perfect bow. Trey slowly bent over Star's neck, and folded the wings to encompass Star's head and neck and they bowed together. While they remained still, no one in the crowd moved, the announcer remained silent, and time stood still.

As the duo rose, the crowd seemed to come alive and together took a deep breath then broke into a thunderous applause. Trey and Star took a full running lap around the perimeter of the arena with wings soaring then turned to exit the arena. As they entered the alley-way, Trey dropped to his horses neck and hugged him and spoke to his stallion with words of gratitude and love. Walking slowly to the stall area, Trey shrugged out of the wings and gently folded them, tucked them under an arm and walked in front of Star to the stall. Breathing deeply, he savored the moment, knowing his vision was complete. What had just been done was exactly as he saw it in his vision, his dream, his goal, and he now felt complete. It was something he couldn't really explain to anyone else, but he felt it within and knew his life had changed. In the ancient times this would have been called a passing over, whether to adulthood or to a special honor, whatever it signified, now it meant he was complete.

Chapter 30: Tribute

TREY TURNED TO SHUT the stall gate but before he could reach for the gate, Skye flew into his arms and wrapped her arms around his neck and hugged him and spoke into his ear, "You were great! Everyone was amazed and couldn't hardly believe what they saw. It was wonderful!" He pushed back to look at her and noticed some of the face paint remained on her cheek as it smeared from his face. With a smile at her new appearance, he said, "What do you mean?"

"Didn't you see the crowd? They were mesmerized!"

"I don't understand, and no, I didn't see anybody, I was a little busy," he replied seriously.

Before she could say more, she was interrupted by the woman that had wished him good luck, last year's champion. "She's right. You were magnificent! I think you just walked away with it all! Good job!" she said as she extended her hand in congratulations. Standing behind her was Trey's Mom and Dad with broad smiles and a few tears. Then came Grandmother and the ladies who gathered around him for a group hug and congratulations and lots of praise. Then Grandmother said, "Of course, if it wasn't for your craft crew, it wouldn't a been nuthin'!" and smiled as if she meant it. As they turned to leave they looked to see the Tribal Council leader approaching with his wife on his arm. He extended a hand to Trey, then waved it aside for a grandfatherly hug for this young man that had brought honor to their people.

Waiting at the back of the small crowd, Trey noticed a familiar figure. He walked over to Mark Blackman and paused, waiting to hear what he had to say. "Uh, I think I owe you an apology. You really did it out there, you showed the rest of us up. All of us with our high-priced horses and fancy gear, some with professional trainers, and you come along and like Skye said, show us how it's done. I was wrong Trey. I shouldn't have called you stupid. If anyone was stupid, it was me. That won't happen again," he stated as he dropped his head. Trey stepped forward and extended his hand, which Mark eagerly grasped in a full hand grasp with thumbs interlocked, then pulled Trey to him as they shared a hug and slapped each other on the back.

"Thanks Mark. That means a lot." Trey felt a hand on his shoulder and turned to see his dad imploring him to return to the crowd. As he turned, he looked back at Mark with an apologetic expression, waved to Mark as he returned the wave and left. Trey's dad said, "They're gonna make the awards soon, son. You might wanna be available." Trey could see the pride in his dad's eyes, something he hadn't seen before, and it brought a special joy to his heart.

The new engraved championship trophy saddle in the back seat provided an arm rest for a very proud Skye as she held the trophy buckle in her hands and asked Trey, "So, are ya gonna get a fancy belt to go with this buckle, cowboy?"

Her comment had interrupted Trey's thoughts that had been knocking at his consciousness for some time. He was grateful for the temporary reprieve and answered her, "Nah. Don't need another belt. I'll probably just put that on a shelf in my room. It's too fancy to be wearin' all the time. Don't want folks thinkin' I'm prideful or sumpin'" he replied.

"I'll wear it for ya' that way you won't have to be worried about bein' prideful," she smiled. She always enjoyed kidding him and now she had more to poke him with. He just smiled and returned his gaze to the window to take in the passing scenery as they left Riverton and headed across the reservation to Ethete and home. For the past several days a nagging thought had been bothering him and now knocked again at his consciousness.

Should I let Star go back to his herd? But the black stallion kicked him out and almost killed him, it wouldn't be safe. But is it right to keep him, he was a wild animal and probably wants to be free. Yeah, but, he was almost killed by a mountain lion and I wouldn't be there to protect him. But do you keep him for you or for him, shouldn't he have freedom? I don't think I could let him go, he means too much to me. I don't know, I just don't know.

THE END

Star Dancer

About the Author

Born and raised in Colorado into a family of ranchers and cowboys, B.N. is the youngest of seven sons. Juggling bull riding, skiing, and high school, graduation was a launching pad for a hitch in the Army Paratroopers. After the army, he finished his college education in Springfield, MO, and together with his wife and growing family, entered the ministry as a Baptist preacher.

Together, B.N. and Dawn raised four girls that are now married and have made them proud grandparents. With many years as a successful pastor and educator, he retired from the ministry and followed in the footsteps of his entrepreneurial father and started a successful insurance agency, which is now in the hands of his trusted nephew. He has also been a successful audiobook narrator and has recorded many books for several award-winning authors. Now finally realizing his life-long dream, B.N. has turned his efforts to writing a variety of books, from children's picture books and young adult adventure books, to the historical fiction and western genres which are his first love.

Discover more great titles by B.N. Rundell and Wolfpack Publishing at:

http://wolfpackpublishing.com/b-n-rundell/

58209918R00116

Made in the USA
Lexington, KY
05 December 2016